COLD TO COMMITTED

Your guide to becoming a top performing
sales development representative

KYLE VAMVOURIS

ISBN-10: 1729798594
ISBN-13: 978-1729798591

Printed in the United States
by Amazon Direct Publishing

Second Edition

I would like to dedicate this book
to my 15-month old daughter, Delphi.
You are small with a big personality.
World, you better brace yourself!

"Character consists of what you do on your third and fourth tries."

James A. Michener

TABLE OF CONTENTS

INTRODUCTION

You may be reading this because you've just started in the world of sales and the position you are starting at is a sales development representative (SDR). Perhaps you're an account executive who wants to keep your pipeline full of new opportunities. You could even be the Vice President of Sales and are looking for ways to increase the production of your salesforce. Whoever you are, I think we can all agree on a common bond:

We want to make more sales!

When I was 21 years old I dropped out of college because I wanted to follow my passion and become a standup comedian. There are few things in this world that give me the experience of euphoria and being on stage is one of them. As you can imagine, my parent were not super excited about this decision, I don't blame them. *Spoiler Alert!* I am not a stand-up comedian and you are still reading a sales book. The balance between advancing my career and doing stand-up comedy was hard for me. I decided to put comedy on hold while I pursued a career in sales.

I first became involved in sales as a membership advisor selling gym memberships at a sports club in a suburban neighborhood (I know… It looks great on a resume). This was my first real experience with overcoming the challenge of "outbound" lead generation. Suburban gyms are very different when compared to city gyms because they don't get as much walk-in activity. Less inbound opportunity means you must go out and create your own.

I would give fliers to local businesses, put them on cars, and hand them out door to door in neighborhoods. I was brought up in an environment of *"torch the land until they come."* The idea was to spread a wide net and repeat this as often as possible with the hope that you would eventually catch a few fish. The best sales reps were the most active, making calls and hitting the streets. I did whatever I could do succeed. That drive led me to my first role in tech sales, a sales development representative (SDR).

That environment was something out of a movie. Hundreds of people in cubicles with headsets on were trying to book meetings and close deals. Employee turnover was high and expectations were even higher. We had a team of around 90 sales development reps all with the same goal—book more meetings. Everyone wanted to get promoted as fast as they could. The only way to get promoted to account executive was to hit the company-defined quota and, it was a real grind.

But...I did it. I worked hard and earned my promotion to account executive. I was an account executive for over a year at that company and then, moved to a startup as part of a group of their early sales hires. This is where I discovered the importance of building and managing a pipeline. Pipeline simply means how a sales person tracks potential clients and where each of those potential clients stand in the sales process.

My first month on the job I booked more meetings as an account executive than the entire sales development team. That team obviously needed help and the company quickly got me involved in their training. This sparked my passion for Sales Development and this is what drove me to write the first version of this book, published in January of 2017.

After a successful book launch, I really wanted to build an SDR team from the ground up. I found an early stage start-up that was looking to grow their sales development team. They had a few reps already, but those reps lacked direction. They didn't have a manager and they were not trained on how to effectively prospect.

I designed and executed a new process, created scripts, and implemented a robust training program. As the team continued to increase in size, I was responsible for training all the new sales development hires. I also continued to improve our prospecting processes for better lead conversion. Our conversion rate went from 3% to 20% and growth was so explosive that it led to a strong series B round of funding.

If my career is the solar system, prospecting would be the sun; poetic, I know. Prospecting is the processes of searching for and scheduling meetings with stakeholders who are part of the decision making process at a company. This is the part of the sales process I love the most. Of course, closing a sale makes me excited. But, there is something very special about speaking with a person who has never heard of your product or service and then, piquing their interest in it. It's repetitive and challenging and, there are not too many people good at it.

I recently read an article about Ali Reda, the man who broke the 44-year-old record for most cars sold in a year—he sold 1,582 cars. To give you context, the average car sales per year for a DEALERSHIP is 1,000.

He said something that really stood out to me:

> *"They would rather deal with someone that's real than just a face on a billboard."*

What Mr. Reda was saying here is powerful. Buyers want to deal with someone real. As technology advances and the manual parts of your job get automated, the last piece left is you—*a human being speaking with another human being.*

That's why it's important that you become a master at having conversations. You must understand how to genuinely connect with other people, because this is what will lead to your prolonged success in sales and life.

In this book I lay out techniques and strategies that you can implement to become a better SDR. My goal with this book is for it to be an aid to help you succeed as a SDR and to lay the foundation on which you will build your sales career.

I know these techniques work; I've used them myself and with my team. This does not mean what I say in this book is the only way to succeed. It is one very successful way. You can experiment with other techniques as well, in order to find out what works best for you.

✓ *Work Hard*   ✓ *Improve*   ✓ *Repeat.*

DISSECTING THE WORLD'S GREATEST PROSPECTORS

Take a magnifying glass to any company and you will see a multitude of different cogs turning and moving each other. Each piece is important and each piece has a place. Without a quality product or service, there wouldn't be a company. Without marketing, the company wouldn't be promoting their products or services. Without salesmen/saleswomen, the company wouldn't have any customers. Arguments about which is the most important cog will be constant, however, they all have one thing in common: They rely on the interest of potential customers, or for the sake of this book, **Prospects**.

Building interest in a product or service is a problem that many start-up companies and small businesses experience. Some will hire teams of **Prospectors** (*Sales Development Representatives*) to scour the internet and reach out to companies they believe are a good fit for their product or service. Here is the classic flow: *find accounts, call accounts, book meetings, find more accounts, book additional meetings. Sprinkle some emails in there, send them a white paper, call them back!*

This process repeats until a harsh lesson is learned; prospecting is hard, time-consuming, and has quite the learning curve. Companies spend a fortune seeking out people to perform the "busy work" of prospecting, but they forget the most vital part: *investing in those people to ensure they develop the skill sets they need to succeed.*

Here is the one of the many things I have learned over the years: *there is no shortage of "good" ideas in sales.* From new tools that focus on finding contacts or sending emails faster, to new scripts that promise to "dramatically" increase conversion, everyone has just the trick to blow revenue out of the water. Don't get me wrong, tools are important and have a huge impact on productivity. My argument is that sales is more about the *people who do it*, than it is about the tech stack they have access to. Many companies throw money at tools instead of education for their salespeople. Because of this, I wrote this book for anyone who wants to learn the basics of how to book a meeting with a cold prospect, regardless of the tools that you have access to.

I have spent much of my professional life studying those who I believe are the best prospectors in the world. I have always felt that if I learned from the best people, took the most effective strategies they had, and combined them with the effective strategies of others, that I would be the stitched-together version of all the best prospectors in the world. It's like Frankenstein's monster that closes a lot of deals, but doesn't get attacked by a village. I set out to learn what the most most successful prospectors do and, it turns out, they have a lot in common (shocker, I know).

Even with the commonalities, each has different methods and way of doing things that they feel work best for them. The first question I'm going to tackle is an important one: what are the habits, beliefs, and activities of the most success-ful prospectors? While reading through these, I want you to take a note of which areas you feel are your weakest, as well as where you feel strongest. At the end of this chapter you will reflect on these and use it for direction on where to focus on improvements.

TRAITS OF HIGHLY-SUCCESSFUL PROSPECTORS

ORGANIZATION

Every exceptional prospector I have spoken with can show me their process down to a "T." They have their targeted accounts organized and their strategy for each mapped out. This is something that doesn't come naturally for a lot of people. Becoming an organized person takes commitment, discipline, and execution. Throughout your sales career you will need to keep track of multiple tasks, all with different levels of priority. Failing to stay organized can cause things to slip through the cracks and could cost you many great opportunities.

Another reason why organization is so important is because you control it. Sales is a world filled with variables that you have no control over, but they im-pact you. A hurricane can cause one of your closing calls to be delayed; a family emergency can cause a meeting to be cancelled. Are you going to let this stand in the way of hitting quota? I hope not...

The variables you can control are the biggest levers you pull to impact your own success. A commitment to excellence in all areas you can control maximizes your chances of being successful month after month, quarter after quarter, year after year.

EFFECTIVE TIME MANAGEMENT

A key component of organization is time management. Sales development reps need to focus on mastering time management first. Booking meetings, follow-up with warm prospects, and sending tailored emails can be challenging to juggle. Even the best sales development reps have missed quota because of just one deal a deal that may have been attained by doing a better job managing time.

ACTIVITY AND PRIORITY BLOCKS

The best prospectors block off their day by activity and priority. They block off times to focus on specific tasks and are selected based on priority and opportunity cost.

For example, suppose 9am to 11am is the best time to make calls because it's when your prospects are most likely to pick up the phone. When you are organizing your day, you should make sure that between those hours you are only focused on making calls, not sending emails or researching accounts. Take a look at an example of how to block off your day.

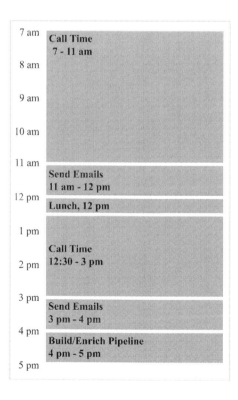

WORK SMARTER

Many people suggest that you should "work smarter, not harder." This is great and all, but why do we have to make a choice? I want to work smarter **AND** harder. Staying organized falls under the "smarter" category—it's mandatory. Mix this with some good old-fashioned work ethic and you have combined the first few ingredients in the recipe for success.

ADAPT YOUR STRATEGY TO THEIR NEEDS

One question top-level prospectors ask themselves often is *"What will it take to get this account from knowing nothing about my product or service to becoming interested in taking a look?"*

This is a powerful question, because in order to get the attention of your target accounts, you must be able to adapt your strategy to their needs. What works for one account might not work for the next. There will be groups of accounts that do require the same basic strategy, but being able to adapt is important. Even more important is knowing when you must adapt.

ASK YOURSELF WHY?

If you ask someone successful at sales development what their process is for booking a meeting, they will likely respond with *"Can you tell me more about the account you're trying to book a meeting with?"* This is because the characteristics of the account being targeted have an impact on how you go about setting a meeting. Because of this, each step of your process needs to be met with the same question: **Why?**

What steps are necessary for me to book a meeting? What does each step do, what's its purpose, and *Why* is it necessary? To be clear, you should have a process that you follow that fits most situations. What sets the best prospectors apart from the rest is their level of understanding and their ability to <u>adapt</u> parts of their process when necessary.

> *I'm not sure about you, but having a constant stream of new accounts sure does get me excited!*

STRATEGY AND EFFICIENCY

Strategy is important when you are generating new accounts. Successful prospectors have a clear process for how they search, enrich, and prioritize. They have drilled this process down to the mandatory components, so no time is wasted. Their goal is to make this process as efficient as possible, and efficiency leads to more potential clients.

DISCIPLINE AND A POSITIVE ATTITUDE

To be successful in sales (I would even argue in life) you must have a strong mindset. There is a lot involved in having a strong mindset but what I would like to focus on are two main traits I see in very successful SDRs (sales development reps). Top performers are *disciplined* and have a *positive attitude, even when times are tough.*

When you lack discipline in any area of your life, it can carry over and impact others. All human beings want to be comfortable—it's ingrained in us. We want to take the path of least resistance to get to where we want to go. The problem? To be successful you sometimes have to take a path of resistance. Success does not always come easy. To make it through the hard times, you must be committed to self discipline.

The hardest part of self discipline is the *"self"* part. The easiest person to lie to is yourself. Lies come in the form of excuses. For example, *"I don't have the time"* is really just your mind telling you *"I don't want to do that."*

I have a trick that I use to help fight the desire to take the path of least resistance. The second I don't feel like doing something, I now *have* to do it. When my alarm clock goes off at 5:30 a.m., my brain sometimes says, *"hit snooze and get another five minutes of sleep."* When this happens I say *"you messed up brain, now we have to get up."*

When I make a commitment to myself, I keep it. Do I mess up? Absolutely. However, I stay reminded of my commitment to follow through on what I tell myself I am going to do. Doing this allows me to course correct quickly when my self discipline slips.

Commit to having a positive outlook. Negativity has the power to stop momentum in its tracks and you cannot afford to let that happen. When you spend every day being disciplined your actions will lead you to success. Don't let negativity drag you back to square one. Negativity comes from internal thoughts as well as external forces.

You Must Avoid Negativity!

AVOID TOXIC PEOPLE

There is a famous anecdote that sat you are the average of the five people you spend the most time with. No truer words have ever been spoken. If you spend your free time with toxic people, then their mentality will infect you. Alternatively if you spend your time with driven people, you will be inspired to push your limits. If you have not removed toxic people from your life, now is the time to do it. It is hard enough to stay disciplined. You can't afford to let the negativity of others hold you back.

TAKE ACTION

Success is a slow process and requires you take action every day. Daily action may not feel like it does much. Will reading 30 minutes tonight really help me book more meetings tomorrow? Maybe not, but finishing that sales book may. The challenge we all face is that it's a lot easier *not* to do something than it is to do it. We all make excuses. If you believe the ones you tell yourself it will stifle your growth.

If you are not growing, you're dying!

POSITIVE AND NEGATIVE IMPACTS

While you're pursuing a career in sales, you will run into many personalities. Everyone you interact with will have an impact on you, your mindset, and even your success. There are two types of impact—positive and negative. Cling to the positive and that will help you grow into a stronger, more successful person. If you get caught up with the negative it will cause you to become stagnant and keep success out of reach. The worst part is you will believe that you are not successful because of anything, other than yourself.

If you don't believe you are in control of your own success, why even try?

KEEP LEARNING

You may have heard of the phrase *"student mentality."* In my opinion this is one of the keys to success in prospecting, and in life. To have a student mentality means to always be focused on learning and growing—never closing yourself off because you *"already know how to do that."* Almost everyone you meet will acknowledge the importance of educating oneself, **but few actually follow through**.

Top performers in any industry are the people who make constant improvement a priority. Obviously, if you are reading this book, you are probably one of the people who make learning a priority. You are already on the right track.

I always recommend reading books and listening to audiobooks about sales. Having a deep understanding of sales techniques will help you become a better prospector. Podcasts and videos are also an option. Sometimes you may find that what you are listening to or reading is too basic for you, however, don't stop. Continue reading or listening with the intention of discovering at least one new thing that you can add to your repertoire. Even being reminded of something that you knew but had stopped doing can be incredibly impactful. That technique, advice, or knowledge can be what propels you to the next level of success.

As someone who has spent a lot of time around sales people, I can confirm that they are very busy. Cold calling, booking meetings, and closing new business deals are just some of the activities that fill up the day. As a result, many people think that they don't have the time to educate themselves. It's the classic excuse, "I'm just too busy!"

Every sales rep should devote at least thirty minutes a day to educating themselves. If you exercise every day, then listen to an audiobook while you do it. You can listen to podcasts during your commute or read part of a sales book before you go to bed. Find the time to add some self improvement into your day—it will have a huge long-term impact.

INDUSTRY KNOWLEDGE

Part of educating yourself should be related to the industry that you are selling, Whenever you are on the phone with a prospect, you must be an authority—that's how meetings get booked. The decision maker will be making a judgment on whether or not you are an authority in the business you are selling to. The more you educate yourself, the easier it is to prove to your prospect that you are providing value and that you have confidence in your service or product. We are trying to convert time into money when we prospect.

You better believe the prospect is doing the same thing.

CREATIVITY

You don't need to be an art major to be a great prospector, but the most successful prospectors are creative. I'm not saying that you need to treat sales as an art, it's not—*sales is a science*. The psychology of how people make decisions has been studied for years. The creativity comes into play when you choose *how* to use sales techniques and *when* you use them.

Because every prospect is unique and communicates differently, the best prospectors can adapt how they communicate to align with who they are working with. For example, if you are speaking with a prospect who values visual explanation, you must adjust your approach to cater to that. If you are working with someone who is very technical and wants to dive deep into the more complicated aspect of your product, you must be knowledgeable in those technical aspects.

There are an infinite number of ways to get the attention of your prospects. It's up to you to be creative when it comes time to set yourself apart. Prospecting will always evolve and change, so use your creativity to push the boundaries.

Not everyone is a solo creative powerhouse. To boost your creativity, I suggest getting a group together for a brainstorming session. The goal is to come up with new ways to reach out to your accounts. What has worked in the past? Can it be improved? What techniques have failed before? Are there any redeemable qualities that can be used in the future? Collaborative energy breeds creativity and this might be the kickstart you need to enhance your own creative thoughts.

Creativity without action is just daydreaming.

The best prospectors do not fall into this trap; they take action quickly. This is because they have another trait that they use when they take action and it leads to improving their processes.

TEST EVERYTHING

Everyone is capable of coming up with great ideas, but if you blindly follow everything you think of, you will end up running around in circles. The best prospectors test everything so they can make an unbiased, data driven, decision on whether it works or not. Test all new ideas and comparing their effectiveness to what you are already doing.

Here's an example of how to do this.

If you want to test a new script introduction, the first step is to decide on what you are trying to accomplish with that introduction. The goal of your introduction should be to get the prospect to have a conversation with you. You would want to track how many times your new introduction leads to a good conversation with the decision maker versus how many times it leads to you getting hung up on. A/B test this, use the old intro(A) on one call and the new one(B) on the next. Repeat this process until you have enough data points to make a decision on which one is better.

Choose one day a week to give something new a try. Spend time thinking about what you are hoping to accomplish by your test. If your current introduction seems to do really well, then you might not want to change it. i.e. don't try to fix something that's not broken. You should only test new ideas if you believe your current introduction doesn't work well or could be better.

Friday "Fun-day" is my day to get creative with my prospecting efforts. This is a day that I test a new idea I have to improve specific areas of my efforts. Get really nerdy about what you are testing and if you stumble on something great, look forward to Monday when you get to implement it across all your accounts!

HAVE PRESENCE

Great prospectors develop something that is very important to their success—presence on the phone. Early in their career, many salespeople struggle to sound comfortable over the phone. In the beginning, most people sound robotic and a little nervous, but most are able to overcome this as they get more confident.

Talking on the phone can be scary at first. This is due to the fact that most of our communication is through messaging and email. As a culture we have become less adept at verbal communication. This affects you and your prospects as well; they may not be super comfortable with phone conversations either. It is your job to be comfortable and to make the person on the other end of the line feel comfortable as well.

Developing your own unique presence over the phone can captivate whoever you are speaking with. If you got cold called by Mark Cuban and didn't know it was him, do you think you would listen? I would argue that you would, because he would have such a unique presence that you would be engaged.

Developing your own unique presence takes time and a lot of repetition. As you get more comfortable on the phone, you will start to see your personality come out.

The fastest way to develop your presence is to simply talk with everyone you can. Strike up a conversation in line at a local coffee shop or talk about the weather with someone who is walking in the same direction you are. Introduce yourself to whoever you can and ask about them. You may feel like you are intruding, but that is just your fears holding you back. If you were waiting to get coffee and the next person in line greeted you, would you be upset or annoyed? I would venture to guess probably not. Humans are social creatures and love connecting with others, but in most cases, fear holds us back.

Some of your prospects may get defensive when you are on the phone with them. They may feel annoyed at first because they think it's just another cold call. However, having a strong presence on the phone can change their mood drastically.

The most successful prospectors are able to connect with anyone because of their unique presence and that makes them enjoyable to converse with.

Don't be afraid to use your personality as much as you can when you are reaching out to your accounts. Don't get wrapped up on trying to "sound professional" and embrace your authentic communication style. Take the time to get comfortable using your personality with everyone you come in contact with. Don't fall into the trap of trying to sound like someone you are not when you are on the phone. Your goal is to sound knowledgeable about the industry and your product or service while maintaining your unique presence. You will come across more authentic and this will allow you to connect with the person you are speaking with on a more personal level.

MOTIVATION

We are all motivated by different factors and you need to find out what motivates you. Is it about making a ton of money? Do you want to get promoted quickly? Make sure you have a clear understanding of what you would like to accomplish. In the world of sales, being able to build a pipeline, engage with prospects, and schedule sales meetings will get you far. Make sure you know where you want to be and how important it is for you to get there. This will serve as a reminder of why you do what you do every day and motivate you to stay disciplined.

CONCLUSION

The above traits are similarities I have observed in the top sales development reps and account executives. I would encourage you to adopt as many of these traits as you can. Becoming great at prospecting will be useful throughout your entire sales career.

At this point you should have some notes on what areas we have covered that you feel confident in and the areas you need the most improvement on.

- ✓ Take a look at your notes.
- ✓ How do you feel?
- ✓ Did you write down a lot of areas that need improvement?

Are you feeling a bit overwhelmed?

This is totally normal. No one has all these traits naturally. They are developed over time.

I want to tell you a story from my time as an SDR.

■■■

I once worked with a sales development rep named John (not his real name, of course). I had been at this company for four months when he started and I was really getting into my groove with prospecting. I had seen much success the last quarter and was constantly helping my peers. My manager put John in my cubicle in the seat next to mine so I could help him ramp up. He was fresh out of college and, like most of us, had never made a cold call in his entire life.

It turned out that John was scared to talk to people over the phone. Everyone is scared at first, but John had this deep rooted belief that calling someone out of the blue was rude and he felt uncomfortable. He felt like he was interrupting someone's life and would often start his calls off with *"sorry to bother you,"* despite my suggestions not to. I worked with John a lot, trying to help him get over this crippling fear. This eventually turned into a deep hatred for the company and the role he was in.

I spent a lot of time thinking about John because on the surface he seemed like someone who would do great. He was smart, really smart in fact. He was funny, personable, and a great conversationalist in person. However, he lacked the ability to use those traits to connect with people over the phone. As a result, John was fired from the company after about three months of far below average results. It was a tough pill for him to swallow, but he understood that the work wasn't the right fit for him.

■■■

The majority of people reading this are in a job where you must book meetings for salespeople who are trying to eventually close a sale. Let me finish this chapter off with some advice that applies to all areas of life:

■■■

Some day you may find yourself in a position where it doesn't look like you can make it.

You may not be able to hit your quota. Maybe your job is on the line and it seems like you won't be able to succeed.

In this moment you have two options. You can put all your effort into

doing whatever you can to achieve success—you can give it 100%. Or...
you can only put in 50%, not your full effort and when you fail you can
say to yourself "at least I didn't try."

The second option is an easier pill to swallow—it protects your ego. It
allows you to make excuses for why you didn't put in that effort and those
excuses mean that it isn't your fault. In my opinion, when you are faced
with this kind of situation, you must ask yourself this: *"What kind of
person am I?"* Do you give 100% regardless of the challenge or only 50%
and protect your ego?

■■■

*Choose to give 100%, even if there is a part of you
that doesn't believe you can succeed.*

Committing to this is you choosing not to fear failure. If you experience failure, learn from it and move forward. You will accomplish more
by committing to being your best self regardless of the situation than you
will by letting your ego take control.

ACCOUNT QUALIFICATION AND GRADING

One thing that's important for SDRs to understand is account qualification. You may work at a company that has pre-qualified accounts for you, which is helpful. Don't let that stop you from reading this chapter. You need to understand *WHY* an account is considered qualified.

You also need to understand account grading and why it will make you a lot more efficient. Anything you can do to optimize the time you spend prospecting is worth it.

Prospecting is a numbers game—the more efficient you are, the higher the numbers you can achieve.

Account qualification is important is because you want to make sure the people you are prospecting are a good fit for your product or service. The last thing you want to do is spend a lot of time trying to book a meeting with a company, only to find that your product or service is not a good fit for their business. Remember, being a great prospector is a lot about time management, and making sure you're spending that time on qualified accounts is vital to success.

THE LIST AND ITS IMPACT ON YOUR SUCCESS

Let's assume you don't already have a list of account qualifications from your company. So, we will need to talk about the possible types of prospecting lists your company may provide and how you will go about qualify accounts. After that, we will talk about grading your accounts, so you can make sure you are maximizing your time. The ultimate goal is to give you a high level understanding of accounts and how you should be thinking about them.

Anyone can blindly call a list. Trust me, you don't want to be just "*anyone*."

LIST VOCABULARY

Flashback to my 5th grade teacher—she loved vocabulary; I did not. It was quite a point of contention in our relationship, I digress. There are some key terms you will need to know.

Account

In sales, account is defined as company, the business establishment that is the source of sales revenue . This includes all information attributed to the company. For example. how many employees they have, their revenue, their website presence, and basics like location, address, and phone number.

Contact

Linked to each account you have contacts, which is exactly what it sounds like. Contacts are people who work at the company. An account might have multiple contacts linked to it, multiple people you can attempt to contact in your pursuit of booking a meeting.

You will have a list of accounts with contacts, either given to you or created by you.

Note: Most CRM systems have the distinction between accounts and contacts built in, so this might be familiar to you.

Dead Accounts

Ahh, the infamous dead accounts—simple and not very exciting. These are accounts that other reps, or you, have worked into the ground. These contacts have gotten an excessive number of calls, and yet, no contact with a decision maker or any of the stakeholders has occurred. These may even be accounts where a previous rep got rejected by a primary decision maker. If you receive accounts like these, it is typically for you to practice the sales workflow and script without much risk of burning a great lead. Usually, you don't expect much from these accounts. Still, if the decision maker said "no" to one of your colleagues a few months ago, that doesn't mean that they are going to say "no" to you!

Web-Scraped Accounts and Contacts

Accounts that are found by searching online are called web-scraped accounts. If you find a contact for an account on linkedin, for example, congratulations! You have a web-scraped contact! These accounts are in their infancy in terms of qualification. All you did was find the company and maybe a contact. You still don't know if they are qualified or even if your information is accurate. It's possible the contact changed companies and didn't update their online profile. Maybe the company downsized dramatically and doesn't have a need for the product or service that you provide. Either way this is your list to qualify, to feed your qualified account list.

Qualified Accounts

These are accounts that you have personally verified. Of course, you might not have a fully qualified account (in the eyes of sale's reps), but you have an actual contact and you know enough to consider the account worth chasing. A list of qualified accounts is where the majority of your meetings will come from (not including inbound or list buys). Your goal as a prospector is to build a large list of qualified accounts so that you always have a list to work.

List Buys

A list buy is when the marketing team pays a company for a list of accounts and contacts. There are a lot of different types of list buys and not all created equal. Ideally, companies on the list are prequalified and may already be interested in the service or product you're selling. This is nice for you because it saves you time trying to create your own list, but, list buys are by no means perfect.

Old Inbound Accounts/Contacts

These are companies or contacts that requested information from your company in the past. There are a few reasons why they might be in your list. The other rep who was chasing the account when it first came in might not have been able to connect with the decision maker. Another possible reason is that it slipped through the cracks and no one reached out to the contact. No matter what the reason, this is a good account because we know that at some point the prospect had some interest in the product or service your company provides. It's your job to discover if that's still the case.

Inbound Contacts

When a contact requests information from your company, it is considered an inbound contact. The main difference between inbound contacts and "old inbound accounts" is temperature. An inbound contact that just came in is just about as hot as a contact can get. You have a specific person at an account that is showing interest—awesome! Sometimes the inbound contact will be at an account you've been trying to schedule a meeting with for a while. Other times it will be a contact from an account that wasn't on your radar. These are considered win, win contacts.

Inbound accounts and contacts are great for helping you hit quota, but don't rely on them entirely. Your quota is there during months with a ton of marketing qualified leads (MQL). That quota is also there when there is a slow month and fewer MQLs.

Your marketing team is most likely focused on driving inbound interest in your product or service. This is fantastic and can really bolster your efforts. That being said, you are held to a quota. Remember, you are the salesperson; you need to generate your own opportunities to hit your quota, make more money, and progress in your career. If you rely solely on marketing, you put yourself at risk of failing to hit your quota at some point.

WHAT ELSE IS IMPORTANT?

COMPANY TYPE
Other than the different account lists that you will receive, it's also important to consider the type of companies you're reaching out to. You want to make sure that when you're searching for accounts and contacts you're finding ones that match the kinds of businesses that can benefit from your product or service. There are three main categories that businesses fall into.

- Small and Medium-Sized Business (SMB)
- Mid-Market
- Enterprise

Your sales workflow is determined by which of those categories your target customer falls into. For example, if you are targeting local businesses, it will be much easier to connect with the business owner than it would be with the CEO of Google. That doesn't mean SMB is better than enterprise at all. What this does mean is that enterprise takes more steps to win and often comes with a higher price tag. Let me give you a quick overview of each of the categories.

Small and Medium-Sized Business (SMB)
Small and medium-sized businesses usually have an owner/operator that manages the day to day and makes all financial decisions. They are smaller companies with smaller budgets and typically less than 50 employees. There is one big advantage of going after SMB—they answer their phones! Thats a big one. As a general rule, SMB decision makers are a lot easier to contact.

Mid-Market

Mid-Market companies can be a challenge to define. Some use number of employees to determine this, typically between 100-1000. Others look at the entire market and find criteria that they use to select the companies that fall in the middle of that market. The reasons why you would want to tackle this market is because they have a larger budget than the SMB, a simpler organizational structure than enterprise businesses, and typically have problems they are aware of and open to solving. The challenge, most likely, is that you're dealing with more than one stakeholder. It won't be nice and easy like SMB. Typically, there will be more than one person involved in the decision making process.

Enterprise

Enterprise businesses are the large companies, the big players in your target market. Think Google, Amazon, Salesforce, and Linkedin. Not every enterprise company will be a household name, but there is one thing that will be true for each—you will need to talk to a lot of decision makers and stakeholders to get their business. As a general rule...the larger the company, the more people involved in the decision process. These companies have over 1000 employees. Managing multiple stakeholders will require a more organized plan, but that is only one aspect that makes enterprise challenging. They also take a long time to win as a customer. The stakeholders involved evaluate multiple solutions and may have to go through several departments to get a purchase approved. The benefit of the additional work you need to get this account outweigh the negatives, because these are usually very high ticket sales. The additional upfront work will pay off.

When reading the overview of each of these categories are you able to identify which one is your primary market? This often isn't as easy as just looking at the business size and asking yourself "which one makes me the most money?" A better question to ask is "which one of these company categories does my product or service help the most?" Your product or service may solve all the problems for SMB but falls short on some features or expertise to benefit enterprise. If that's the case, winning enterprise level deals will be challenging to near impossible and not worth the time. Think about where your product or service has the most impact and start there.

QUALIFICATIONS

Now that you've determined which type of company you should target, ie: SMB, mid-market, or enterprise, you need to understand what the qualifications are to be a good fit for your product or service. Your company most likely will have a list of qualifications that they've identified, but if you have to do this yourself you should take a look at your current customers. Ask yourself, *"What do these companies all have in common?"* For example, a large portion of your company's customers might be a certain type or industry, such as ecommerce, software, or the restaurant businesses. If your company provides services for software organizations, target your account search towards software organizations. If your service benefits restaurants, search for restaurants. Pretty simple, right?

There is more to qualification than just what industry the company is in. Let's say you are selling software that helps restaurants manage staff. Would you want to find a list of all restaurants? **No way!** You will spend a lot of time calling small, family-run restaurants who don't have a problem managing their employees. This is why you need to add some qualifications so you don't waste your time calling accounts that won't benefit from your product or service, or worse, booking a meeting with them.

Here are some examples of qualifications you may want to consider if your company doesn't have a list for you.

- How many employees?
- How much revenue?
- Funding round
- Technology already being used
- Industry
- Current workflow
- They already spend money on an area that your solution helps with
- The company has a specific department
- Location
- Who is the best contact?

LOCATION MAKES A DIFFERENCE

An important part of your qualification is location. It narrows your account search and helps make your list more focused. In some cases your company may have you assigned to a territory. You may be restricted to Manhattan or all of New York, for example. If you have a territory make sure you know your exact boundaries, often identified by area codes. If you don't have a territory, then you'll need to find a place to focus your initial work.

Here are some criteria to use when choosing your own location (if you have a territory feel free to skip this part):

Where are your products and services most popular?

The first thing that you need to determine is where your products and services are needed/wanted the most. Many times this will be near the main location of the company, but that's not always true. Think of what parts of the country have a lot of businesses that use your product or service. If you are selling to tech companies, for example, you might consider San Francisco, California, Austin, Texas, or Seattle, Washington. If you're selling a product to help farmers you might want to contact a different location.

Where are most of your current clients located?

Another way to narrow down your location is to find a city where you have a large clientele already using your product or service. Write a list of the 3 places in the country that most of your customers are located. They might serve as a reference or a case study to use with prospects local to them. For example, if you are talking to the owner of an auto dealership in Chicago and are able to use one of their competitors as an example of how effective your product or service is, you may have a higher chance of getting that meeting.

Where are you located?

Sometimes the best place to prospect is in your own backyard. Are there groups you can join? An association? Club? How about networking events in your industry that can give you access to decision makers? Don't discount the power of meeting someone at a bar who happens to work at a company that you've been trying to connect with. They might be the missing piece to getting the decision maker on the phone and ultimately booking the meeting.

WHO IS THE BEST CONTACT?

When qualifying an account, the contacts you want to meet with are a very important qualification. There is a chain of decision-making authority in every company. The problem is that the title of the person doesn't always tell you what their role is. For example, if you are selling call-center software, you may be looking for the Director of Customer Support. This might be the best point of contact for most of the companies you call. In some situations, however, it might turn out that the director of customer support only deals with the day to day of his department, not the technology that they use. That would make him a stakeholder, not the decision maker.

The difference between a stakeholder and a decision maker is one of authority. Stakeholders are people at the company you are trying to book a meeting with who have influence in the decision, but do not make the final say. The decision maker is the person who has the final say. That being said, it's no uncommon for the decision maker to require the involvement of stakeholders before making a decision.

Let me give you an example that should make this easier to understand.

■■■

Bill is the CEO of ABC company. You are trying to book a meeting with ABC company, but Bill is very busy and doesn't reply to your emails. Sarah is the Director of Customer Support and much easier to connect with. You call and find out from Sarah that she has some frustrations with their current call-center software. She tells you that Bill will also need to take a look at your solution because he has the final say. You ask if Sarah and Bill would both like to be on the first call you're scheduling, but Sarah and Bill's calendars don't line up. You end up booking a meeting with Sarah.

■■■

Your question...Is booking a meeting with Sarah the right thing to do?

You probably got the answer right—Yes it is. Here's a follow up question... *Why is it the right thing to do?* This can be a little harder to answer, so, I'll help. Sarah is a stakeholder who has a problem with their current setup, a problem that you happen to have a solution for. You can't get in touch with Bill—you've already tried. Getting Sarah to endorse your solution is necessary to get a meeting on Bills calendar. It is definitely worth your time to show Sarah your product.

Top to Bottom
When you are trying to figure out the best contacts for your product or services, work top to bottom. Who is most likely the ultimate decision maker? Once you have the title of that person, work down and figure out all the people who are possibly involved in the decision—the stakeholders. You should have a list like this (let's stick to the call-center software example):

- CEO
- Director of customer service
- VP of sales
- Customer service manager
- Sales manager

Once you have your list you're going to make another one. What are the aspects of someone's job that makes them a decision maker or a stakeholder? That list should look something like this:

- Controls budget spending
- Is an administrator of the current call center software
- Leads a team that uses the call center software
- Works with the main decision maker

Once you understand the titles and the criteria that makes up your decision makers and stakeholders, you won't spend your time prospecting contacts who aren't involved in the decision making process.

ACCOUNT GRADING

Now that you understand what makes an account qualified, it's time to talk about how to prioritize. It is very important that you give your accounts a grade so that you focus more of your efforts on the accounts with the highest probability of yielding results. Just to clarify…this is not necessarily a "lead score" or "account score" that you already have associated with your accounts. If you have a marketing team that scores your accounts you may not have to grade them yourself, lucky you! Often times marketing will use multiple criteria to give every account a score. The better the score, the more likely it is for that account to convert into a meeting and ultimately a customer. Without this to help you prioritize accounts it's going to be important that you give them a grade yourself.

I use is a simple ABC grading scale (real academic of me I know). In order for you to grade accounts you need to have a clear definition of what each letter represents. The main reason why this is so important is that, based on the criteria, some accounts will get more of your attention than others, possibly even different forms of outreach.

The criteria that you use to determine which letter grade an account gets will be based on your own unique situation. You may want to use data quality, i.e. did you find a contact with an email and phone number? Does this account have a website? You might even use qualifications that we spoke about earlier in this chapter—the more qualified the higher the grade. Here's a breakdown of accounts that fit each particular grade. It will be your job to identify criteria that you will be using.

A Accounts

"A" accounts are companies that you feel are the best fit for your product or service. You have a contact with a phone number and email. You believe that if you spoke to the decision maker of the account, you would feel confident in demonstrating the value of your product or service and book a meeting easily. These are the accounts you should spend the most strategic time on. Working an "A" account requires more careful planning, so be very selective when assigning an "A."

B Accounts

You will quickly learn to love these! "B" accounts are the companies that you feel are "just ok" and the ones you will work the most. On the surface they look good, but you don't have the information that you need to comfortably put them in the "A" category. Maybe you have a contact at that company, but don't know if they are a stakeholder or not. You may not have the time to spend customizing every letter of every email to them like you would for your "A" accounts. That being said, this is where you will find more accounts worthy of the "A" grade.

C Accounts

"C" accounts are those that you have limited information on or that you haven't been able to qualify yet. You might only have the company name and website, but no contacts or any really helpful information. These accounts are good for testing your outreach. You can cold call them and test a new pitch, or try sending a new email campaign to see how the email analytics are. With more research you may get enough information to up their grade to a "B." Think of these accounts as needing research.

You don't want to scour the internet during peak call hours to see if you can find a contact at a "C" account, but don't count them out completely. They may surprise you. One day you will get a phone call from a business owner who received one of your email campaign emails and they want to take a look at your product or service.

Remember: "C" accounts aren't junk. They are just the accounts that you don't have enough information on to know if they are likely to convert. Your goal in calling and researching these accounts is to bump their grade up to a "B" or to "A." A typical workflow might look like this:

1. Find accounts
2. Grade them all "C"
3. Call your "C" accounts and do some research
4. Move their grade to "B" or "A" accordingly

WHALE HUNTER? A SHOCKING TWIST!

There is actually one more letter I recommend assigning to accounts—"W". W is short for *whale hunting* (please don't actually hunt whales—they are peaceful creatures!). These are the companies that would make your quarter look superb if you could book a meeting with them. They are businesses with big names, with great logos, and might be considered a booking "pipe dream." You should not spend much time on these accounts, but consider them an exciting side project.

The probability of winning the business of a "W" account is so low it isn't worth spending too much energy on them. That being said, chasing these is a blast and gives you the opportunity to be creative. Happy hunting!

CONCLUSION/OVERVIEW

There it is folks—account qualification and grading. There are a few things that you need to answer to ensure that you got the most out of this chapter.

✓ What type of account list do you have today?
✓ What kind of company are you prospecting?
✓ What makes an account qualified?
✓ What are your top locations?
✓ What are some of the best contacts to speak with about your product or service?
✓ Are you committed to grading your accounts?

This whole chapter is fundamental. Odds are that you are pursuing a career in sales because you enjoy talking to people and solving problems. To be successful in sales you must be able to manage your time well. Understanding what a qualified account looks like and grading those accounts will help you reduce the amount of time you spend on low value activities.

I want you to be the best prospector at your company. In order to be that you must put your full focus and energy on the accounts that will yield results. Some of you might be saying "but Kyle, how do I find accounts?"

Read on young grasshopper... Read on.

BUILDING AND MANAGING A PIPELINE

WHAT IS A PIPELINE?

I know you're itching to put down this book and start calling. I get it; I love the hunt as well. Before we dive into call technique, I think it's important for you to understand what a pipeline is and how to build and manage one. Fair?

A pipeline is your entire list of accounts, from new accounts you haven't touched to ones that you're "sooooo close" to booking a meeting with. Typically, your pipeline consists of all your accounts unless you remove them from your list.

Building and maintaining a pipeline is a lot of work and should always be part of an effective salesperson's workflow.

The main areas we will cover in this chapter are how to find accounts and contacts to add to your pipeline, enriching those accounts, and finally, how to stay on top of your pipeline. Building and maintaining a pipeline is a lot of work and it can get pretty mundane. The biggest mistake you can make is to neglect your pipeline maintenance, because you're too busy or you think you already have enough momentum.

Even if the company has a powerful marketing strategy, building and managing a pipeline will always be part of a salesperson's workflow.

This is what separates the best prospectors from the rest.

PROPER ACCOUNT ORGANIZATION

Account organization is the first step in successful pipeline management. The best prospectors stay organized. They organize everything—their days, accounts, contacts, and outreach. Keeping these areas organized is extremely important and will directly impact your success.

For the process of managing your pipeline, I recommend using stages. A "stage" is what identifies where each account is in the sales process. Here are 6 stages I recommend—"Open," "Working," "Prospect," "Bad Data," "Archive," and "Unqualified." Think of these as "buckets." Buckets are put in to track account status. Following this stage system from the beginning will help you effectively manage your prospecting time for meeting bookings, reaching out to interested contacts, and adding accounts to your list. Most customer relationship management (CRM) systems have various ways to to mark these stages and track them.

Let's go over the above stages in detail.

Open

Accounts marked as open are ones you haven't attempted to contact. These are new accounts and are not qualified yet. They may be missing a contact or important information like a phone number or email. Once you find that information and call or email a contact at this account, it gets changed to the next stage.

Working

Working is the next step in the accounts circle of life. Much like a caterpillar spinning its cocoon, a Working account is where change happens. These are the accounts that you have correct information for and are regularly pursuing. Some of these accounts you already know are qualified; others, you will be attempting to contact for qualification. Your list of Working accounts will be where you spend a good portion of your time, especially in the beginning of your prospecting. This will also be the stage where most of your accounts will live and they will live there until you make contact or change their stage.

Prospect

An account is in the Prospect stage when you have spoken to a contact and they are qualified. They might not be ready, but they are a good fit and may need your solution in the future. Whenever you speak to a contact, your goal should be to book a meeting. That isn't always possible. If the decision maker says that they are not interested or you find that your information is bad and this isn't a qualified account, you will remove them from this stage. If you have a reason to call this account again, it stays in the Prospect stage. Be selective about the accounts you put in this stage. If you only spoke to a receptionist don't put the lead into the Prospect stage. It should be left in the Working stage. If you spoke to the director of marketing and he tells you that they are in need of a solution like yours, the stage is definitely Prospect.

The last three stages (Bad Data, Archived, and Unqualified) are for accounts that are no longer in your active group. You can consider these leads "removed" from your pipeline. Never delete them because conditions could change and you or marketing might want to try and activate the accounts again.

Bad Data

This is for an account where the information you have is bad. The phone number might be disconnected and you can't find another one. Emails you send them bounce. This stage is where you might want marketing to take over and try and enrich for you. Or, you can do it yourself during non-peak calling times.

Archived

If you have never been able to contact a decision maker or they've told you they are not interested in a way that warrants you taking them out of your pipeline, the account should be marked Archived. Use good judgment and only put accounts here that you have no future plans for recontacting. Always add a note why the account has been archived.

Unqualified

If you learn something about an account that makes it no longer qualified, you should mark it as Unqualified. Sometimes we think an account is qualified based on what we find in our research or what we hear from the employees we speak with on the phone. As you chase these accounts you may learn something that no longer makes them worth chasing. For example, if you only work with companies that use Salesforce as their CRM and in your research you find that they are using Salesforce, you have a qualified lead. If you talk to a decision maker and he says that they just switched from Salesforce to a different CRM, you would now mark that account unqualified.

Take a look at this diagram that shows how account would flow between the different stages

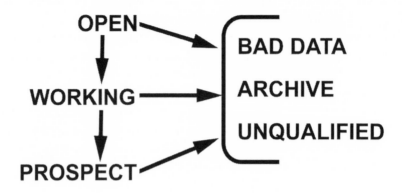

FINDING LEADS

Alright friends, now we get to the good stuff. How do we find leads to call? How challenging it is to find accounts and contacts really depends on two things—the tools you have available and the types of businesses you are targeting. Some companies invest a lot into software tools that aid their sales development teams, but not all companies do. I will write this chapter from the perspective of someone with no prospecting tools. I will label each section with the tools that would make the section I am writing about either automated or obsolete. If you would like, skip the sections in this chapter that are irrelevant to you based on the tools your company provides. The one tool I will assume you have access to is a CRM (CRM is a "customer relationship management" software that tracks your accounts and contacts to keep them organized).

BUILDING YOUR PIPELINE
(Tools that may help: LinkedIn, Sales Navigator, Zoominfo)

In order to build your pipeline you need to know what you are looking for. Make sure you know the qualifications that we went over in the last chapter. When it comes to building your pipeline, efficiency is key and you want to add accounts quickly so you can start your outreach. It is common for new reps to spend a lot of time doing research trying to find out as much information as possible. Most information can be found by making one call, and that saves you time. There are four mandatory pieces of information that you are looking for—contact name, company name, company phone number, and company website.

You will notice that I do not mention contact email and there's a reason for this. The first wave of prospecting is just finding the basics to add accounts to your pipeline. I am a firm believer in organizing your time in tasks that are similar in nature. Research shows that context switching slows you down, so I recommend avoiding it whenever possible. That being said, there are some secondary pieces of information that can be easy to find while you're looking for the 4 mandatory pieces of information above. Those are contact title, contact email, company email, and any qualifications that may be easy to find online, for example, number of employees.

If you see information while searching for the mandatory 4 pieces that is useful to you, add it. However, do not fall into the trap of going out of your way searching for information that isn't mandatory. That information may be hard to find or not available and all you will end up doing is wasting time.

To find potential accounts look online for lists of companies that fit in your target market. For example, Yelp.com would be a great resource if you are selling to restaurants. If you are selling to tech companies who just received series B funding, check out Crunchbase.com. Simply Google some criteria and find companies that match that. Once you have the company name, find their website and there you will see their main phone number. Now you have three of your four mandatory criteria, the last piece being contact name.

Many company websites have a section where they list their team. Finding a contacts name can be as simple as going to that section and choosing the person who is most likely to be the decision maker. If the company website does not have that section simply google "CEO of ABC Company" and you will most likely find it. LinkedIn is another great resource for finding contacts but you will get blocked from the site if you make too many searches, unless you pay.

As you find this information you should be adding it to your CRM system and putting the account in the Open stage. Repeat this process until you have at least 100-300 accounts in your pipeline, depending on your industry. You will keep coming back to this process as you need more accounts to call, but 100 accounts should be enough to start with.

At this point you should have a list of at least 100 companies, each with a website, phone number, and a person who you would like to get in contact with. So what do you do? I would get on the phone and start calling. You will learn more in less time by calling than by playing around on Google, but that doesn't mean we are done building your pipeline. You aren't going to be able to get your desired contact on the phone every time so you will need to use other forms of communication, like email or LinkedIn message. In order to use these other forms of communication you will have to continue to enrich your accounts.

ENRICHING YOUR ACCOUNTS
(Tools that may help: Zoominfo, Discoverorg)

Enriching your list requires you to spend time doing deeper research on your accounts. The goal is to find information that will help you get in contact with a stakeholder, which will get you closer to booking a meeting. This information is email, LinkedIn, direct phone number, and a second contact. Which one of these is the most effective depends on your target market. For example, if you are targeting tech companies, LinkedIn may be even more powerful than Email. This doesn't hold true in industries where LinkedIn is less popular, for example, construction. Fortunately, email is universally used, so it's a great place to start.

Email
Finding the email of a contact at the company you are working can be a challenge without any tools to help you. The first thing you should do is call the company and see if you can connect with your target contact. If you are unable to reach that person ask the person you speak with for the email you are looking for. This is the gatekeeper. A gatekeeper is the person who answers the phone and screens calls. They most likely won't give you the email, which isn't surprising considering their job is to prevent you from speaking with the contact. I have come across a few tips that have been useful for finding someone's email.

Tip #1: Ask the gatekeeper if you can send them an email with some information to show your target contact. If they agree and give you an email, such as *firstname.lastname@companyname.com*, then you've struck gold. You can use the same email format with your contacts first and last name and that will most likely be their direct email.

Tip #2: Look at social media pages and sometimes, in the about section, there will be an email. That email will either be a generic *info@companyname.com* email or it will be the email of whoever created the page. That email will give you the format which will allow you to do the same thing as tip #1.

Tip #3: Good old fashion guessing! Nothing screams fun like sending emails to different format variations hoping that one sticks. There are a few websites that allow you to type in an email address and it will tell you if that email is valid or not. This is a slow way to figure out someone's email and I would recommend you ask your company to invest in a tool before spending too much time on this.

LinkedIn

If you are targeting an industry where the employees use LinkedIn, then you would be foolish to ignore this medium. Sending someone a message on LinkedIn is more likely to get you a response than email, so take advantage of it. LinkedIn offers a premium service that, if you pay for it, will help you find accounts and organize your contacts. It will also allow you to send them a message without being connected. If you don't have access to LinkedIn Premium then you will have to send your contact a connection request.

I recommend connecting with every one of your contacts on LinkedIn. That way you will be able to send them a message without LinkedIn Premium. When enriching your accounts, find your contacts LinkedIn page, and then, save the link to their profile. Their LinkedIn page will give you insight into your contact that will help you customize your messaging for all future communications.

Direct phone number

It can be a bit of a challenge to find someone's direct phone number, but not impossible. The easiest way is when you are calling a main company number and they have a directory that gives you the extension of your contact. Not all companies make it that easy, and of course, then you will have to ask the gatekeeper. If the gatekeeper won't give out that information, you only have one more option, other than using a tool. You can send an email to your contact hoping that they respond and have a direct line in their email signature. After you have exhausted those avenues, just stick with the company's main line. We will talk about how to get through gatekeepers in the next chapter.

Second contact

Finding a second contact at the company is helpful when you're not getting any traction with your first contact. You want to build out the second contact with the same information as the first, contact name, email, LinkedIn, and a direct phone number. You will be attempting to connect with this person using similar methods as the first. The reason why this is important is because it's not uncommon for the first contact you find to be hard to reach or not the correct person. By having multiple contacts at a single company, you are maximizing your chances of finding an entry point, a person to start a conversation with.

One of the easiest traps to fall into is spending too much time doing research.

There is a point where research goes from invaluable to a time waster. With few exceptions, you should aim to be able to enrich your leads in two minutes or less. Do not trick yourself into thinking that the more research you do the better your calls will go—that's not how it plays out. A call will go as well as your skill level allows it to go and more research rarely helps. More research can help when customizing an email and we will cover that in a later chapter.

TRIGGER EVENTS
(Tools to help: LinkedIn Premium, Owler)

When a company goes through a big change, or has something interesting happen it can trigger action. So many events can trigger someone to take action, even something as simple as a conversation at a party. In most cases you will not know when these events take place involving the contacts that you are trying to book a meeting with. However, there are public events that correlate with action being taken and these are called trigger events. You want to make sure that they pop up on your radar so you can take advantage of them and reach out to the account.

News
Great prospectors stay up to date with what's going on in their industry, since this gives them authority and also alerts them to trigger events. You must take the time to find what blogs your target contacts are reading. Subscribe to relevant newsletters and join the LinkedIn groups they are members of. You should immerse yourself in the world of the people you are going to be selling to. This will help you learn the language that they use, and to understand their challenges on a deeper level. It will give you more to talk about when engaged in conversation.

In addition to industry news, it is also important to keep up to day with what's going on with your accounts. The more up to date you are, the more likely you are going to spot a trigger event. You should set up a Google alert for your prospects or use a tool to notify you when something hits the news about one of your accounts. If one of your accounts reveal a new feature or receives another round of funding, you should be one of the first to hear about it. This kind of information gives you a reason to reach out to the account. Customizing your communication with this info shows that you are well informed.

Side note: The news is also a great way to find new accounts that you may have missed during your search. Subscribe to news sites that cover your industry (such as TechCrunch if you target tech companies). Get in the habit of reading the headlines every day. If you see some news about a company that you believe could be a good fit for your product or service, add it to your pipeline.

Job change

One of the benefits of being connected with your contacts on LinkedIn is that when they get a new job you will be notified. If they left their company, that means that they must be replaced. A new hire who is taking on a role that makes them a stakeholder or decision maker in your sales process is a great trigger event. When someone is new to their role they have a strong desire to make an impact and this makes it a great time to introduce them to your product or service.

Hiring spike

If a company is going through a sudden increase in hiring, it can indicate momentum. With an uptick in momentum and the desire to hire a lot of people, there is also a lot of focus on taking action and making internal improvements. This is a trigger event that you can use to reach out and show how your product or service can help the company achieve better results.

CONCLUSION

Building a pipeline can be tedious, especially if you lack the tools necessary to make this process much faster. It can often feel like you are spending a lot of energy for a seemingly small result. My strong recommendation is when things are going well, you need to double down on efforts to fuel your success in the future. What do I mean by this? Sales tends to be cyclical—some months are great, others horrible. However, the best salespeople are the most consistent. So, how do they accomplish this? *By being consistent in their effort.*

It is so easy to let off the gas when you hit quota early. So, here's my question for you...***when you hit quota a week before the end of the month, what will you do?*** Will you keep your energy up and focus on feeding your pipeline with new accounts? Or, will you start taking days off, or having long, off-topic conversations with your coworkers during peak calling times? It is so important that you keep prospecting, keep pushing forward, this is how you build and keep momentum. That momentum will make you a lot of money and propel your career in sales. Stay on the gas, don't let up and get "comfortable."

Maintaining your pipeline is mandatory; you want to keep it healthy. Feed it new accounts, enrich those accounts, and stay in tune with trigger events. Being a great prospector is about discipline. It's about sticking to your process, even when you want to take a break from the busy work. In sales there is hunting and gathering; this chapter was about gathering. The next step?

Grab your spear. It's time to hunt!

THE IMPORTANCE OF AUTHORITY AND
HOW TO GET PAST THE GATEKEEPER

In this chapter we are going to cover the importance of authority and your ability to deal with the many different personalities you will interact with in your quest for sales success.

When I began my career in sales I started as an SDR at a large tech company, I was wide-eyed and excited for the future. You might be experiencing this now; you are about to start at a great company with good benefits and are ready to pound the phones and make something of your life. Here is the best advice I can give you before diving into actual skill sets:

Act with Authority!

Before you dial that first number, you must understand a very powerful aspect of cold calling—authority. Authority can be the difference between repeatedly having to call back because the decision maker is "busy" and speaking with them on the first call.

What exactly does it mean to have authority? It means having confidence when you speak, knowing that you are calling to bring value, not just to try and sell them something. Authority is also being educated about your target customers' industry and the problems they face.

Authority comes from your tone of voice and rate of speech. Everyone who talks to salespeople often can tell if they are good or not within the first few seconds. If the person you are talking to you senses that you are weak, you have already lost.

I learned the importance of authority very early in my sales career. The new territory assignments were up and I could hear sighs of relief around me because my colleagues didn't get assigned their most feared territory—New York City.

Guess who didn't get to sigh with relief? This guy. I was so nervous. Everyone said that people in New York City were rude and the territory was very difficult to sell into. Remember when we spoke about not letting negativity get into your head? This is pretty much why.

Want to know the truth about New York City, the Big Apple? There are some whip-smart business owners there who don't want to waste time on people who cant help them grow their business. They don't have patience for sales people who lack confidence in themselves or their product or service. Thriving in this territory requires authority and having that authority over the phone made me a better SDR. It will make you one too.

Every time you pick up the phone, speak with authority!

It does take practice. Below are some tips that I have found helpful in sounding more confident.

Tip #1: Belonging

Tell yourself that you belong there. Have you ever heard those stories of people who get into restricted areas just because they had so much confidence that no one stopped them? Remind yourself often that you are not bothering anyone with your call, that you belong on the phone with the decision maker. This will help you sound more confident and speak with purpose.

Tip #2: Stand up!

If you find yourself sounding weak over the phone, then stand up when you're talking. If you're like most people, standing will make you feel more powerful and that will translate over the phone.

Tip #3: Stop using soft language.

This one can be challenging because we are all programed to use words that make us sound weak, kinda, maybe, sort of, like, um…just to name a few. Listen to your call recordings and find out what you say that comes across as low confidence and write them down. Put these words on a sticky note and stick it to your monitor as a constant reminder to stop saying those words. You will start to become more aware during your calls and you'll be able to reduce your use of words that make you come across as someone with low confidence.

Tip #4: Speak with confidence

No matter who you're speaking to, speak with confidence. This will require a constant effort to change the way you speak naturally. If you have trouble speaking with authority when on a call, force yourself to speak with confidence and authority everywhere you go. Go on, tell that Chipotle employee that you want guacamole! In all seriousness, this will help you get comfortable speaking with authority. If you want to come across confident and authoritative over the phone, act as if you are a confident and authoritative person.

THE GATEKEEPER..."ENEMY" OF THE SALESPERSON

The gatekeeper is the dreaded enemy of the salesperson. Your goal will always be to talk to the decision maker or stakeholder at a company. The gatekeeper is the person who will do everything in his or her power to stop you from doing that.

It's a classic power struggle and this interaction alone will eat some great salespeople alive. Getting past a gatekeeper takes practice, authority, and even a bit of misdirection. At a high level, your main objective, when speaking with a gatekeeper, is to control the call. All gatekeepers have their own script that they use to handle a cold caller. They will ask you questions and you will answer those questions, but you most likely won't speak with the decision maker.

You will run into a lot of different gatekeeper personalities throughout your career in sales. Getting past the gatekeeper is not always going to be easy, but dealing with them is part of the gig. Be confident. Keep calling. The more calls you make, the more confidence you will have. Never stop calling because you encounter too many gatekeepers. Every dial makes you a better SDR, a better salesperson.

GETTING PAST THE GATEKEEPER

A gatekeeper is the first line of defense the decision maker has. They rely on them to stop people who call asking for them with the intention of pitching a product or service. Your goal is to get through the gatekeeper and to the decision maker as quickly as possible. The goal of the gatekeeper is to stop you. In this section, you will learn how to interact with the gatekeepers, how to get through them, and what to do when they give you trouble.

The first thing that you must understand about gatekeepers is that they speak to cold callers multiple times a day. They know what someone cold calling sounds like and oftentimes default to "can I take a message?" If your goal was to leave a message, this would be great, but your actual goal is to book a meeting with the decision maker. Knowing what gatekeepers expect to hear when speaking with a cold caller will allow you to sound different, which can throw them off.

Your objective is to have a short conversation with the gatekeeper giving them as little information as possible. Before we go into the script, let's talk about the different types of gatekeepers you will run into. There are three main types—the college student, the lifer, and the office manager. Each comes with their own nuances.

The College Student

This type of gatekeeper is exactly what the title suggests, a young person who answers the phone for the business. These people are in no way professionals when it comes to screening cold calls, so this makes them the easiest gatekeeper to get through. Think of yourself when you were in college, and the jobs you had. Odds are you were trying to do a good job and please everyone; you didn't want to make a mistake. The advantage you have when dealing with this kind of gatekeeper is having confidence and speaking with authority because it has the greatest impact on them.

The Lifer

The next type of gatekeeper is similar to the college student except that they have more years under their belt:. I call these gatekeepers The Lifer. They are more likely to interrupt your script than the college student is. Having authority is important but with this kind of gatekeeper you may want to build some rapport as well. A playful joke goes a long way with The Lifer, because you want to relate to them. If you have ever been in the service industry, you know what it's like to feel underappreciated. Appreciating The Lifer is often the key to getting through to the decision maker. Just don't go too far off script. If you can't get through to the decision maker, remember that The Lifer tends to know a lot about the processes within their company. They also may not be as secretive as The Office Manager, so they can be a great resource for finding out information about the decision maker and the business itself.

The Office Manager

This Office Manager gatekeeper will be the most challenging one to get past. I call this type of gatekeeper The Office Manager, because even if that isn't their official role, it's what they feel they are. This type of gatekeeper has no problem trying to bully you off the phone once they sniff that you are cold calling. They may even ask you what you are trying to talk with the decision maker about, only to follow up with "I handle that." Trust me, many do not "handle that." Later in this chapter we will cover a few strategies that you can use to get through this kind of gatekeeper.

One thing to always keep in mind—most offices have more than one gatekeeper. If you keep running into The Office Manager and they won't let you through, try calling back at different times. The College Student may be the one to pick up and let you through to the decision maker.

YOUR GATEKEEPER SCRIPT

Every salesperson has a script, one that they use on a cold call, and throughout the sales process. One area that tends to get overlooked is the interaction with the gatekeeper. This is because it seems easy on the surface—ask for the decision maker; if they aren't available call back. Having a gatekeeper script you stick to is very important. The interaction with the gatekeeper is short and there are less variables to consider. Because of this it's easy to get a sense of how most gatekeeper conversations go and write a script to optimize for that conversation.

The first part of the script is your introduction and this alone can get you through the gatekeeper and to the decision maker. Don't be fooled by the simplicity, there is a reason for every word.

You: **Hi there. I'm looking for Jim! [pause] It's Kyle.**

This intro is all about the delivery, so you need to practice. You need be upbeat and sound like you're the decision maker's friend, "Hey, I'm looking for Jim!" You will notice [Pause] as the next part of this intro. You want to leave a one to two second pause right after the first part. The reason is the gatekeeper is programmed to ask "may I ask who is calling" when someone calls wanting to speak with the decision maker. By giving a pause before saying your name you are giving the gatekeeper time to process who you are asking for and trigger their programed response, which is to ask your name. As their brain tells them to ask your name you are giving them your name, throwing them off a bit and forcing them to pivot quickly.

Often times the gatekeeper will not be able to pivot and they will ask you your name, the one you just gave them. This may cause the gatekeeper to feel a bit embarrassed, much like saying "you too" when the ticket vendor says "enjoy your movie!" That embarrassment can lead to the gatekeeper transferring you to the decision maker instead of asking you more questions. Dare I call it gatekeeper judo? I dare.

Now, what if your intro doesn't get you right through to the decision maker? In this scenario you will have to navigate the gatekeeper's script. Read the dialog below between a gatekeeper and an untrained SDR trying to speak with the decision maker, Jim.

SDR: **Hello, I'd like to speak with Jim**

Gatekeeper: **May I ask whose calling?**

SDR: **My name is Devon**

Gatekeeper: **What's this regarding?**

SDR: **Your call center software. It's my understanding that Jim handles that.**

Gatekeeper: **Yes. He's in a meeting right now. I can send you to his voicemail.**

SDR: **That would be great.**

Now that gatekeeper deserves a promotion! What you read above illustrates what the gatekeeper is trying to accomplish every time. In the next section we are going to talk about how you can control the call, break the above conversation flow, and increase your chances of getting passed to the gatekeeper and to the decision maker.

GETTING THE GATEKEEPER OFF THEIR SCRIPT

Your best chance of getting passed *any* gatekeeper is to force them to break away from their usual script. In the majority of cases, if a gatekeeper transfers you to the decision maker, it's because they made a mistake. The gatekeeper can't make a mistake if they are following the script that they use every time someone calls. You need to control the conversation and the best way to do this is by asking questions. If you ask questions, you're in control of the conversation and you are forcing them to react to you.

EFFECTIVE GATEKEEPER HANDLING TECHNIQUES

There are three main techniques to taking a gatekeeper off their script—the interrupt, the back pedal, and talking over their head. The effectiveness of these techniques varies based on what kind of gatekeeper you are speaking to.

The interrupt

What you are doing with this technique is responding to their scripted question with a close ended question that they will naturally respond to. Once you get the response to that question, you interrupt the gatekeeper so they can't get to their next scripted question. Your interruption gives the gatekeeper some context that makes them assume that this might be more important than a cold call call. Let's take a look at an example.

Gatekeeper: **May I ask who is calling?**

SDR: **It's Kyle; is Jim with a client? [Close ended question]**

Gatekeeper: **Yes, where... [We got our answer and cut them off before their next scripted question]**

SDR: **Shoot, I missed him. That's my fault. I should have called earlier, Lets see…. When's a better time for me to call back?"** *[This gives the impression that you are busy executive, not a cold caller, which will compel the gatekeeper to answer honestly]*

The dialog above requires good delivery. You need to sound disappointed in yourself for missing Jim. You also need to make it sound like you're looking at your calendar when you say "let's see…." You are setting yourself apart from the 99% of cold calls this gatekeeper screens. Because this conversation has gone so different from the norm, the gatekeeper is more likely to give you a callback time. Get the gatekeeper's name and call back at the time they gave you. Address the gatekeeper by name and they will remember you and may put you right through to the decision maker..

The back pedal
This technique is for when you need to reverse the gatekeeper's initial perspective of you. If you get the feeling that you have irritated the gatekeeper, you want to do your best to build empathy to correct the situation. Showing that you are human and make mistakes can turn a call around. Take a look below.

Gatekeeper: **May I ask who's calling?**

SDR: **It's Kyle. Is Jim with a client?**

Gatekeeper: **Yes, where...**

SDR: **Shoot, I missed him. That's my fault. I should have called earlier. Let's see…. When's a better time for me to call back?"**

Gatekeeper: **You interrupted me. I was asking you what company you're calling from.** *[The gatekeeper is frustrated with us]*

SDR: **I'm so sorry. I'm calling from ABC Company. I'm embarrassed**

because I had a note to call Jim back at 1 and I'm running behind. What time would you suggest giving him a call back? *[People don't want other people to feel embarrassed and we are hoping by saying this and following up with some context we come across less like a cold caller and more like someone who is a bit flustered because th*ey are running behind]

This technique works well on The Lifer and even better on The College Student. The Office Manager may not entertain your request for empathy, so this might not be the right way to go with them.

Talking over their head

If you're speaking with a gatekeeper who is asking too many questions and want you to speak with them instead of the decision maker, you can use this technique. Talking over their head simply means asking the gatekeeper a question that they will not be able to answer. This will show the gatekeeper that the purpose of your call is more in depth than they can handle. When the gatekeeper doesn't understand what you're talking about, they will assume it's important and may transfer you to the decision maker. Take a look at the interaction below.

> Gatekeeper: **I handle the CRM system here. What can I help you with?**
>
> SDR: **Great! I was just calling to verify something. When you installed the CRM system, did you fully integrate the marketing automation platform? This would have been done in the back end of the system?**
>
> Gatekeeper: **Uh, you know, I'm not too sure.**
>
> SDR: **No problem. My records show that Jim is the person who set up the system. Is he in a meeting?**

As you can see, we asked the gatekeeper a specific, technical question that even the decision maker might not know the answer to. For you to use this technique, your product or service would have to have an element that's complicated or not commonly understood. This technique works very well with The Office Manager.

HOW TO KNOW WHEN TO LET GO

It's important for you to also understand that you can't win every battle; sometimes it's just not in the cards. You may find yourself chasing a contact for months only to fail to get through the gatekeeper. Don't feel bad giving that account to a coworker, especially if they are able to get passed that gatekeeper and book a meeting with ease. You may be surprised to find out that the missing piece was a different voice. For example, a gatekeeper might have a negative association with people who sound "alpha" over the phone. All you have to do is give that lead to a "sweet" and "charming" coworker and they will melt that gatekeeper's heart like rainbow sherbet in the hands of a four-year-old during a California summer.

Your time is valuable
Don't waste it chasing contacts that won't convert. However, don't just give up on an account because it's a little hard. You need to be honest with yourself. Don't get rid of an account because you don't feel like putting in the effort. If you get the feeling that you aren't getting through because of something out of your control, like how your voice sounds, then let it go. Remember that song from Frozen, *"Let it go, let it go! Turn away and slam the door."* (See that, I referenced the movie *Frozen*, and we are talking about cold calling…)

Come on! That's good stuff!

Leaving a message
"I can take a message" is one of the most common phrases you will hear from a gatekeeper. The decision maker could be right next to them, but once they smell a salesperson, a simple, "Can I take a message?" will be used to shut you down. Don't worry, all hope isn't lost! There is still an opportunity to set yourself up for a conversation with the decision maker. The first technique is misdirection—agree with them and pivot. Take a look at the example below.

Gatekeeper: **Can I take a message?**

SDR: **Yes, [pause] Actually I'm going to be in and out of meetings today and I'd prefer not to play phone tag. When would be a better time for me to call back?**

The use of the pause here is functionally the same as the pause that we use in our introduction. You want the gatekeeper to hear you say yes, start to shift their brain to message taking mode. When you pivot, the gatekeeper will have to quickly pivot with you and this is when you are more likely to get the truth. If you don't sound like a typical salesperson, the gatekeeper may give you a better time to call or even transfer you on the spot.

You may be asking yourself, "Why don't I want to leave a message?" Well, you may be planning on calling that contact tomorrow, or later that week. Assuming the gatekeeper is giving that message to the decision maker, which is not always the case, this will create a paper trail. In the vast majority of cases, decision makers will not call you back when you leave a message with the gatekeeper. Sitting and waiting for a call is not the position that you want to be in. You always want to be proactive and that means you have to be the one calling back.

There will be times when you are forced to leave a message and there is a way to maximize your chance of getting a call back. First, let's think about what is happening on the other end of the line when you are leaving a message. The gatekeeper is going to get your name, company, and then ask you what the call is regarding. As you reply they will be listening and writing down what they think they need to relay. Let's take a look at the massage many untrained prospectors leave.

Gatekeeper: **what's your name?**

SDR: **Kyle Vamvouris.**

Gatekeeper: **Where are you calling from?**

SDR: **ABC Company.**

Gatekeeper: **What's this about?**

SDR: **Tools for marketing that help with X, Y, and Z.**

Gatekeeper: **What's your phone number?**

SDR: 777-777-7777

That isn't likely going to inspire someone to call back, is is? What I suggest is taking control of the note taking part of the conversation. When you explain what the call is about give enough information to force the gatekeeper to pick what to write down. By doing that they will key into words that they feel are important, which the decision maker reading their note may feel is important as well. Let's go through an example.

SDR: **Sure, I can leave a message. Do you have a pen?**

Gatekeeper: **Yes.**

SDR: **Write this down. My name is Kyle Vamvouris. I'm calling regarding your customer support software. Jim set it up. My number is** 777-777-7777.**"**

Here is how the message will most likely come out:

Kyle

Our Customer Support Software

777-777-7777

This message is vague and may get the decision maker to call you back. The gatekeeper might still ask you some questions like, "Where are you calling from?" Simply answer them and ask a question in return. Here is an example.

Gatekeeper: **Where are you calling from?**

SDR: **From ABC Company. Is your company still using software X to manage your inbound support tickets?**

Gatekeeper: **Yes.**

SDR: **Ok, great. I appreciate your time today.**

You should try to avoid leaving messages as much as you can because the response rate is typically very low. If you received messages from salespeople every day how many would you call back? However, you may find yourself in a situation that requires you to leave a message. Make sure to keep it short, vague, and call them back. Never sit around waiting for a response—that's a recipe for failure.

Leaving voicemail

Occasionally, you will be asked if you would like to be transferred to the decision maker's voicemail. I'm a fan of voicemails so long as you aren't leaving one every time you call. Many times voicemails are left unchecked or may get deleted before the message is finished. Because of this, I believe it's important to leave something brief on an infrequent basis. Let's take a look at an example of an untrained SDR leaving a voicemail.

SDR: **Hi Jim, this is Kyle Vamvouris calling from Forusall. I'm calling because I believe we can help make your support team more efficient with our software. Give me a call at** 777-777-7777.

This voicemail doesn't inspire the prospect to give you a call back. There are two types of voicemail scripts I think do a good job, I call them Mysterious and Valuable.

Mysterious voicemail
The goal of this voicemail is to pique the interest of the prospect enough to motivate them to call back. You want to give as little information as possible, but enough to build some emotion. Take a look at the example below.

> SDR: **Hey Jim, it's Kyle Vamvouris. I called your customer support line and there are a few things I noticed that I felt were worth calling you about. Again, it's Kyle Vamvouris from ABC Company. My phone number is 777-777-7777; that's 777-777-7777.**

This voicemail is short and easy to create for any product or service. After saying your name you go right into a short observation to build up curiosity. Once we have the prospect's interest, we give them our name, company, and phone number. The reason why we are not giving our company name in the beginning is because that's what most of the sales voicemails they get sound like, let's not be like "most."

Valuable Voicemail
The valuable voicemail script is about saying how you can help and asking for a call back or a referral. We want to explain a little about how we help, and offer the decision maker to pass us on to a stakeholder. Let's take a look at an example and then go through why it works.

> SDR: **Hey Jim, it's Kyle Vamvouris. Im reaching out because it seems like your support team may be getting overwhelmed with tickets and this increases wait times for your customers. We've had a lot of success in solving this problem. Again my name is Kyle Vamvouris from ABC company. My number is 777-777-7777; thats 777-777-7777. If you're not the right person to speak with about this, feel free to connect me with that person.**

This voicemail starts with the problem that your product or service solves. By starting with this you will capture the attention of the decision maker who is aware that this is an issue. You then mention that you've had success solving this problem. This gives the decision maker context about what you do and why you're calling them. At the end of the voicemail we ask for the referral. This is because the person who we are leaving this message for might not be the best person for us to speak with and we would like that person to connect us with who is. This shows that we aren't trying to be pushy, that we really want to help and, we want to make sure we're helping the right person.

Not all your voicemails will be the same. Sometimes you have to improvise and that's totally ok. For example, if you've left the decision maker a voicemail a week ago and plan on leaving another one, you might not want to use the exact same script. Experiment with your voicemails and track success. Stumbling on a solid voicemail with a high callback rate can be the key to blowing out your quota.

Always Learn Something New
If you don't get in touch with the decision maker, that's fine. Many people who make cold calls believe the only value of the call is to book a meeting. I would argue that if you sit down to make cold calls with only that goal, you are missing something very powerful. The information you are able to gather from the gatekeepers, stakeholders, and decision makers is invaluable. Your goal should be to learn something new from every call. The last thing you want is to spend a month chasing a lead only to realize that the company isn't even a good fit for your product or service. You may even discover that the company is planning on evaluating solutions like yours in Q1 when they have the budget.

Take Notes
I always recommend writing down bits of information you believe could have an impact on your outreach efforts. Every time you call an account, ask whoever you speak with at least one of your qualification questions and write down their answer. This gives you ammunition for when you get in contact with the decision maker. Imagine how much credibility this line gives you… "I spoke to Susie at the front desk and she told me X, Y, and Z. Can you give me some insight on how you're tackling these today?"

CONCLUSION

The gatekeeper is the first line of defense and is an area of frustration for a lot of prospectors. Using the techniques I have laid out in this chapter, you will greatly improve your chances of convincing the gatekeeper that you aren't just some punk making a cold call. Show them that you are a person of value and make sure to treat them with the same level of respect you are expecting from them. Gatekeepers are people too. You both are crossing paths, so don't be afraid to engage in some witty banter. Don't spend all your time talking with gatekeepers but don't be dismissive of them either.

AN EXERCISE IN SUCCESSFUL GATEKEEPER MANAGEMENT

Start writing down which category you would put each gatekeeper you speak with in. Getting passed each different type of gatekeeper gets much easier with repetitive experiences. Each industry has quirks and you will master the necessary techniques with time. Always keep a record of your calls and their results.

Practice, Practice, Practice

Success takes practice, so don't let a rough call with a gatekeeper bring your mood down and effect the rest of your productive time negatively. Always stay focused and do what I do when a call goes south. I say to myself "on to the next" and I pick up the phone and make another call. So, with that said...

On to the next!

EVERYTHING YOU NEED TO KNOW
ABOUT COLD CALLING

Cold calling is one of the most dreaded aspects of sales. Salespeople hate it so much that some are even fired because of their own lack of effort in this area. Some say that the key to cold calling is having a great script. As if you can say a bunch of words in a specific order that will mesmerize the prospect and book a meeting. Of course, having a script is important and you should be able to book some meetings just by reciting it. However, in order to reach the high levels of success with cold calling you must be comfortable going off of your script and using more advanced techniques to get your message across.

Some of you might think that cold calls are old-fashioned and unnecessary in today's world of sales. Personally, I love the lie that *"cold calling is dead."* It means there is less competition on the phones. If you get hired at a company where none of the sales reps make cold calls, you have an opportunity to be the top SDR in three to six months just by picking up the phone and cold calling.

That being said...

I wish I could tell you that reading this section of the book would be enough to transform you into the best cold caller on the planet. There are so many variables on each call that it is impossible for me to cover all of them, I'll do my best to give you the basics and then some. There will be key fundamentals that you can tailor to your own product or service that will help you be more comfortable with what to say when you're on the phone with a prospect.

LEARN ABOUT THE PROSPECT

You should know that you aren't the only SDR calling the type of prospects you are targeting. To set yourself apart you need to be able to relate. Spend time learning about your target prospect. I recommend that you reach out to a few people who you would consider decision makers at companies similar to the ones you are targeting. Ask if you can take them to lunch or coffee and learn about their day. Here are some example questions you can ask.

✓ What does your average day look like?

✓ What are some challenges that come up frequently?

✓ Can you tell me a story about how you overcame that challenge?

✓ What is your favorite part of your job?

✓ What is your least favorite part of your job?

✓ What is something that you do that you feel is important but doesn't get noticed?

✓ How many cold calls do you get?

✓ What are the majority of those calls regarding?

Learn as much as you can about your prospects. This way you will be able to relate to them over the phone.

LEARN THEIR WORLD

You want to know what words they use and how they talk with each other. Subscribing to their newsletters and joining their groups will help you gain a stronger understanding of their world. Understanding them better will make you better at speaking with them over the phone. After you have a high level understanding of your prospects world, you can start to call them.

STRUCTURE OF THE COLD CALL

Every cold call is different, which is why it is so important that you adapt to every scenario. Still, there is a basic structure that most calls follow.

- the introduction
- the path
- find the gap
- close the gap
- ask for the meeting

Here's an overview in detail.

THE INTRODUCTION

The first make or break moment in any cold call is the introduction. If you fail to capture the attention of the decision maker during the introduction, you will lose the opportunity to explain how your product or service is a business solution for their company. I believe a cold call is about buying time. Every word you say is either costing you time with the prospect or buying you more time. The introduction is the most important part of a cold call because you have not "purchased" any time yet. Let's take a look at an introduction that fails with the decision maker.

> SDR: **Hi. My name is Kyle Vamvouris and I'm calling from XYZ Company. XYZ Company is the leading provider of marketing software designed to organize your leads by quality and score them with a custom algorithm. Do you have a moment for me to explain what we do and see if it would be a good fit for your company?**

Does this introduction sound compelling? Do you think that a director of marketing would like to hear the rest of the pitch? I am going to go out on a limb here and say that the answer to both of those questions is **no**.

When you begin a call, the main objective is to get the prospect to commit to speaking with us, even if it's just for a short time. We do this by asking for some of their time in exchange for some potential value. Here is an example.

> SDR: **Hi Sarah, this is Cody calling from ABC company, how are you today?**
>
> Prospect: **I'm doing well.**
>
> SDR: **That's great to hear, I'm reaching out to you specifically as the person who runs the marketing team for your company. I'm not sure we can help each other, but I thought it was worth a quick call. Do you mind if I ask a few questions and let you decide if we should chat?**

Let's break this down.

> Line 1: **"Hi Sarah, this is Cody calling from ABC company, how are you?"**

This might be the most controversial, and widely debated sentence in all of sales theory. The debate on whether you should ask how the prospects day is has been going on for decades and I have a very simple take on it. When I greet someone I ask them how they are. I don't feel the need to change that just because it's someone I don't know and I have the intention of introducing them to my product or service. There are some downsides to asking how the prospects day is going and also for not asking, so that makes it a wash in my mind. Test this approach to decide what makes you more comfortable.

Line 2 & 3: **"That's great to hear. I'm reaching out to you specifically as the person who runs the marketing team ."**

The reason why we say this is because we want the prospect to know that we're not just calling for anyone. We've done the amount of research necessary to know that he or she is the person who actually has the authority. Finding out that someone is the director of marketing is not a breathtaking achievement, but the power of knowing this information plays directly into the words we are choosing to say.

"I'm reaching out to you **specifically** as the person who **runs the marketing team**." Those words stand out because they are precise and come across as thoughtful. Saying "runs the marketing team" is very different than saying "director of marketing" because it sounds as if we know more about their role than just what we see in our customer relationship management (CRM) system. This part of the intro is worded to communicate that thoughtfulness and authority.

Line 4: **"I'm not sure we can help each other, but I thought it was worth a quick call. Mind if I ask you a few questions and let you decide if we should chat?"**

This part of the introduction is the most powerful. We haven't given the prospect any context about what the call is regarding, but we are alluding to the fact that we may be able to help. The desired effect is to pique the interest of the prospect, get them to think "maybe we can help each other?" Our follow up question is giving them the illusion of full control of the call, "Mind if I ask you a few questions and **let you decide** if we should chat?" When you phrase this question like this you make it very easy to answer yes.

You may be wondering why I said that this gives the prospect "the illusion" of control of the call. The reason why this is just the illusion of control is because we know that there are really only two main responses to our question, either "sure" or "what's this about?" Both those responses are basically the same; they are asking you to continue. The answer "no" is unlikely because the prospect doesn't have enough context about what this discussion is about to be able to confidently reject the call. Of course, you will occasionally have a prospect answer "no" and often, that will be followed with a brush-off. Overcoming brush-offs will be covered in detail later in this chapter.

The Path

After we get the prospect to agree to let us ask a few questions, we get to the part of the script that I call The Path. Take a look at the example below.

> Prospect: **Sure**
>
> SDR: **Thanks for the time. I'm calling from ABC Company. We help marketers increase market qualified leads by automating the qualification process, improving targeting, and tracking return on investment. Most folks I speak with are focused on improvement. Is that the same for you or are you more focused on tracking other areas such as ad spend?**

The objective of this part of the call is to give the prospect some context about how we help and let them give us a direction to take the call in. To create your own path first you should come up with at least three features and/or benefits of your product or service. Once you have those the next part is finding two focuses that your prospect is likely to have and that you are able to help with. In the example above the first focus we use is *"improving the quality of their market qualified leads,"* because the marketing director is likely to be focused in this area and our solution will help. The same applies to the second focus we mention in the example. We are trying to spark a conversation and set ourselves up for the most important question on the cold call.

Why?

When the prospect chooses one of the two paths that you gave them, you now have the opportunity to ask "why is that important to you?" The answer to this question will give you the ammunition you need to book the meeting. Let's continue with our example.

> SDR: **Thanks for the time. I am calling from ABC Company. We help marketers increase market qualified leads by automating the qualification process, improving targeting, and tracking return on investment. Most folks I speak with are focused on improving the quality of their leads. Is that the same for you or are you more focused on accurately tracking the return on your ad spend?**
>
> Prospect: **I would say the main focus for me right now is on improving the quality of our leads.**

> SDR: **I hear that a lot. I'm curious…why is that a main focus for you currently?**
> Prospect: **Well, recently the conversion rate on our leads has dropped. We're not sure why this has happened, but I'm working on figuring it out.**

We've learned two great pieces of information from the prospect's answer. We've learned that their current marketing qualified lead conversion has dropped, and that they don't know why. In this example, we will be able to use what we've learned when we ask for the meeting, because we are offering a solution to a problem they have. However, we are not ready to ask for time on their calendar. Before we do that it's necessary to understand what they are trying to achieve and this is something we do in the next part of the script.

Finding the gap

Once we know what the prospect is concerned about and why it's their main focus, we can determine what it is they are trying to achieve. This is called finding the gap. We are trying to identify a gap between where the prospect is today and where they would like to be. Let's continue with our example below.

> Prospect: **Well, recently the conversion rate on our leads has dropped. I'm not sure why this has happened but I'm working on figuring it out.**
>
> SDR: **You said that your MQL conversion rate dropped? Where is it at now?**
>
> Prospect: **35%, last I checked**
>
> SDR: **Where would you like to see that number?**
> Prospect: **My ultimate goal is 65%, but back up to 55% would be great.**

What's nice about this example is that we are now talking numbers. The prospect wants to be at 65% conversion and today they are just at 35%. That's an easy gap to discover. Sometimes you're not able to find a numerical gap and that can make it challenging to use this technique on the fly.

Here is a good way to think about it. What's the current situation and what would you like the situation to be? Here is another example.

> Prospect: **Well, recently the conversion rate on our leads has dropped.**
>
> SDR: **Why did your conversion rate drop?**

Prospect: **I haven't been able to figure that out yet.**

SDR: **Why is that?**

Prospect: **We have qualified leads coming in from a lot of different sources and it's a tedious process to sort through them all.**

As you can see, we are still able to find a gap even though we are not working with numbers. In the above example the gap we found is that the prospect is having trouble identifying why lead conversion has dropped. Always try to quantify this if you can. If you can't, finding the gap to discover where the prospect is and where they want to be can still apply. Once we understand the needs of the prospect we can shift our conversation to solving their problem.

Close the gap

So far, we've learned the prospect's focus, why it's a current focus, where the company is now, and where they want to be. The next natural place to go is determining what they're currently doing to solve their problem. Let's continue with our original example.

Prospect: **Well, recently the conversion rate on our leads has dropped. I'm not sure why this has happened but I'm working on figuring it out.**

SDR: **You said that your MQL conversion rate dropped? Where is it at now?**

Prospect: **35%, last I checked**

SDR: **Where would you like to see that number?**

Prospect: **My ultimate goal is 65%, but back up to 55% would be great.**

SDR: **What are you doing now to get your conversion back up?**

Prospect: **Nothing yet, because we don't know what's causing it.**

Our prospect has now admitted that in order to improve their lead conversion rate they need to figure out what is causing the drop. That takes us back to asking our favorite question:

Prospect: **Nothing yet, because we don't know what's causing it.**

SDR: **That makes sense, but I'm curious...why are you having trouble figuring out what's causing the drop?**

Prospect: **We have leads coming in from a lot of different sources and it's a tedious process to sort through them all.**

SDR: **Is that problem still on your priority list?**

Prospect: **Yes.**

Ask for the meeting

Now we have everything that we need! The prospect admitted that there is a problem, expressed the challenge they have trying to solve that problem and that the problem is still on the priority list. At this point it's time to move to my favorite part of the call—asking for the meeting.

> Prospect: **We have leads coming in from a lot of different sources and it's a tedious process to sort through them all.**
>
> SDR: **Is that problem still on your priority list?**
>
> Prospect: **Yes.**
>
> SDR: **Since this is still a priority for you, why don't we set aside 15 minutes tomorrow and I can walk you through how we've helped other folks improve their data reporting across multiple marketing channels so they can more quickly identify problems and focus their time on improving their lead conversion. Does tomorrow at 11:00 am work?**
>
> Prospect: **That works.**

We did it—we booked a meeting! When we ask for a meeting, we're tailoring it to their problem, and offering them a solution. We position our close as something other folks have been able to do. This is because we want the prospect to know that they are not alone and this is a problem that can be solved. Finally, we give them a time instead of asking for one. It is very important to be assumptive because it removes a lot of uncertainty in the meeting setting process.

You may be thinking that this example is making it look too easy. If you think that, then I have some news for you...*You're right!* This is a very optimistic example of a cold call, one that I created to illustrate the high-level call structure. We can't script every single variable, so for the rest of this chapter I am going to introduce you to some techniques that you can use in specific situations.

COLD CALLING TECHNIQUES

Every call is going to be different and require you to think quickly and adapt your strategy on the fly. You will encounter this frequently, so it is important to be prepared for the situations that come up most often. The goal of this section is to arm you with some basic techniques that I have found to be effective.

OVERCOMING THE BRUSH-OFF

As you are making calls, you will notice that early in the call many prospects will give you an excuse for why they don't want to talk with you. These come in various forms and I call them brush-offs. A brush-off is the prospect saying something in an attempt to end the call before they know what you are calling abour or even enough to decide whether your product or service could be valuable to them. A quick note...this is not the same as an objection. An objection typically comes at the end of the call when the prospect knows what your product or service is and has a reason why they do not want to continue the conversation.

Before we talk about how to overcome a brush-off, we must first fully understand what they are. Every company will get a different set of brush-offs based on their industry, product, or service. The words the prospect says may be different for you than it will be for someone else, but the sentiment is the same, "I don't feel like speaking with you right now." Let's take a look at some examples.

- "Im not interested"
- "I'm too busy to speak about this"
- "Send me an email with more information"

You must have thick skin to cold call and this is why. These brush-offs are responsible for 90% of all frustrations salespeople have with cold calling. Fortunately, you know they are coming so you have plenty of time to prepare. There is a simple technique that can insure that you will be able to respond to any brush-off that is thrown your way. It is called the **Triple A**. Triple A stands for *acknowledge, answer, ask.*

- ✓ **Acknowledge:** Let the prospect know that you heard them
- ✓ **Answer:** Address their underlying question or concern
- ✓ **Ask:** Follow up with a question to regain control of the call

Let's use "I'm not interested" as an example.

Prospect: **Not interested**

SDR: **I totally understand, Terry, I called you out of the blue and my intention is to see if it makes sense for us to have a conversation. Most folks I speak with are focused on improving the quality of**

their MQLs. Is that the same for you or are you more focused on accurately tracking the ROI on your ad spend?

Re-read the example above and break it down by acknowledge, answer, and ask. Once you do that keep reading for the correct breakdown.

- ✓ **Acknowledge:** I totally understand Terry, I called you out of the blue.
  (We are acknowledging the fact that their lack of interest is directly related to our cold call.)
- ✓ **Answer:** My intention is to see if it makes sense for us to have a conversation.
  (We are answering the underlying concern that the prospect has—that we are going to try and sell them something.)
- ✓ **Ask:** Most folks I speak with are focused on improving the quality of their MQLs. Is that the same for you or are you more focused on accurately tracking the ROI on your ad spend?
  (We are asking an open-ended question, in this case giving them the path, in order to regain control of the call. The goal is to get the prospect talking with us, not telling us that they aren't interested again.)

Let's take a look at another example.

Prospect: **Send me an email with more information.**

SDR: **Sounds good Terry. I'll email you by the end of today. I have a lot of information I can send, so I want to make sure I send over something relevant. Most folks I speak with are focused on improving the quality of their MQLs. Is that the same for you or are you more focused on accurately tracking the ROI on your ad spend?**

Break down this response like you did the other, by acknowledge, answer, and ask. After you do this take a look below for the correct breakdown.

- ✓ **Acknowledge:** Sounds good Terry, I will send this email over by the end of today.
  (We are acknowledging that they asked for an email and are agreeing to sending it.)

✓ **Answer:** I have a lot of information I can send, so I want to make sure I send over something relevant.
(We are answering the underlying concern that the prospect has—that what we are calling about isn't something that they need.)

✓ **Ask:** Most folks I speak with are focused on improving the quality of their MQLs. Is that the same for you or are you more focused on accurately tracking the ROI on your ad spend?
(We give the prospect the path in an attempt to get a conversation started.)

Take some time to write down all of the brush-offs you get when cold calling. Select the most common three and follow the Triple A structure to write your own response to each. You should practice reciting your responses every chance you get, so you are crisp and confident when you say them on the phone. Here is a game you can play with some of your coworkers. Grab a ball and sit in a circle. The person with the ball will say a brush-off while bouncing the ball to a random coworker. That coworker must respond to the brush-off while catching the ball. The idea is that the ball bouncing towards you simulates the pressure you feel on the phone when the prospect brushes you off. Repeat this until everyone can respond to every brush-off from memory, without stuttering, and with confidence.

ON CALL ALARMS

When you are in a conversation with the prospect, it can sometimes be difficult to know where to go next. This typically happens because the prospect is talking a lot and giving you a lot of information. Your challenge is figuring out what to do with that information, and how to capitalize on it to book a meeting. Regardless of how a call is going you must be listening for on call alarms. An on call alarm is a statement made by the prospect that indicates one of three things.

✓ They have identified that something can be improved
✓ They have taken some kind of action to improve something
✓ They need clarity on if a problem exists.

At first, it may be challenging to identify these, but as you practice, on call alarms will be so blaring that they will be like... *an alarm!* The first question we have to answer is how to identify on them. I have broken this down into a simple acronym, N.W.A. Those of you who are a fan of late 80s hip hop will have no problem remembering this one. However, my abbreviation is very different than what you are used to. N.W.A. stands for *Need, Wish,* and *Action.*

Need

Need is the most powerful word that the prospect can say. If your prospect needs something that you can provide, then you, my friend, are most likely booking a meeting. To be honest, this is the least common on call alarm. It also doesn't always come up as the prospect saying the word "need." Sometimes it is baked into the context of what they are saying. Take a look at the following examples.

> Prospect: **I need to figure out what has caused the MQL conversion rate to drop.**

> Prospect: **I have spent a lot of time on this and can't seem to figure out why the MQL conversion rate has dropped.**

The first example is the easy one to identify—they said the word "need" and your alarm bells should be ringing. The second one, however, can be a bit trickier to identify. They don't use the word "need," but they are expressing the need to figure something out. "Need" is baked into the context of the sentence. You will improve at identifying needs as you practice and have more conversations under your belt. The next part of N.W.A. is the W, and this one can be tricky as well.

Wish

Wish is slightly more common than need, but a little bit harder to identify. This is because you don't often hear a prospect use the word "wish." Because the word won't come up often, it will require you to get good at identifying it within the context of the conversation. Let's take a look at an example of a prospect with a wish.

> Prospect: **I shouldn't have to spend so much time in Excel, but it is what it is.**

This falls into the wish category because there is no evidence that this is a need for the prospect. However, you can tell this is something that they simply tolerate...something that they wish they didn't have to do. Wish is a powerful, because the prospect is admitting that they are frustrated with something and that frustration can motivate them to book a meeting.

Now let's talk about the "A" in N.W.A. This comes up the most frequently.

Action

It is safe to assume that the decision maker you are speaking with has taken action at some point in their career. Odds are, they take action all the time to improve the business. Because taking action is required for growth, this is typically the most common on call alarm you will experience. Lucky for you, it's also the easiest to identify. Take a look at the example below.

> Prospect: **I just started looking into the drop in MQL conversion last week.**

The fact that the prospect has decided to take an action is important to us. It's important because for action to take place there must be motivation. In order to book a meeting, we need to understand what is motivating the prospect and why it is so important. If the prospect has taken an action, it typically means that there is something that they need to accomplish, something that your product or service can help them with.

Ok, so you've identified an on call alarm. It's ringing loudly and you're excited because this is the moment that will change the course of the call and will lead to a booked meeting! What do you do? Well, it's similar to what you would do if there was a fire alarm and you were actually on fire...

STOP, DROP, & QUESTION!

The reason why I call these on call alarms is because they alert you to ask a follow-up question. Your focus, after hearing an alarm, is to dive in and learn more about that specific part of what they said. The beauty is that this gives you a path to booking a meeting, and this is exactly what you need on any call. So, what follow-up question do you ask? Take a look at a few examples.

- Tell me more about that.
- What motivated you to do that in the first place?
- What are you trying to accomplish?
- Why is that important to you?
- Why are you trying to figure that out?

The simple way to think about this is that you are digging into the "why" behind their need, wish, or action. Your goal is to get the prospect to open up and tell you about their challenges. When you understand their challenges, then you can tailor the rest of the call and book a meeting on a solution. Let's take a look at an example of how this might play out.

Prospect: **I just started looking into the drop in MQL conversion last week.**

SDR: **What motivated you to do that?**

Prospect: **I had a conversation with some of the sales people and they said that the quality of the leads have gone down and I need to verify this.**

SDR: **What have you found out so far?**

Prospect: **Nothing. Everything looks the same to me, but a lot of this data is hard to gather.**

SDR: **You said that you need to verify if the salespeople are right about the quality...why is that a main priority?**

Prospect: **Because I need to know the cause, so I can fix it.**

SDR: **Is figuring this out still a priority for you?**

Prospect: **Yes.**

SDR: **Since this is a priority for you, why don't we set aside 15 minutes tomorrow and we can walk through how other folks have been able to improve their data reporting so they can more quickly identify problems and focus their time on improving their MQL conversion. Do you have time tomorrow at 11:00am?**

Prospect: **Yes, that will work**

In this example we had two on call alarms. Can you spot them both? "I just started looking into the drop in MQL conversion last week" is an example of action. The SDR, in this example, asked a great question and the prospect said that they "need to verify this" which is another, stronger, on call alarm. Understanding what problem your prospect needs solved is how you are able to tailor the rest of the call in a way that positions your product or service as a solution. Listen to one of your call recordings and see if you can spot the on call alarms. Did you notice it when you were on that call live? Did you stop, drop, and question? Hopefully, as you listen to your call recordings and make listening for N.W.A.s a priority, you will improve on your ability to identify on call alarms.

FEEL, FELT, FOUND, FOLLOW-UP (FFFF)

This next technique is a framework that will help you overcome objections, transition topics, and build credibility. The feel, felt, found, and follow up (**FFFF**) will also help you come across more natural over the phone. This technique can be used at any point in the call, which makes it very versatile. The idea is to relate to your prospect, express that they are not alone, and explain that others have been successful. Let me explain each piece of this process and then show you an example of it all together.

Feel

The first part, feel, is very simple. We want to relate to the prospect and show empathy by expressing our understanding of the situation that they are in. The reason why we do this is because it shows the prospect that we care about what they are going through. It also hints that we know about their industry, because we aren't surprised to hear that they are facing this specific problem. Here's a simple example.

> SDR: **I know how painful that can be.**

Felt

The next part of the FFFF is the felt. We are going to give the prospect example of someone else in their same situation. You want to use an example in a similar industry or with the same job title. Our goal is to reinforce the fact that they are not alone and follow up with a description of the problem they are facing.

> SDR: **A lot of marketing directors I speak with share the same frustration. They need to find the cause of a problem and in order to figure it out, they have to gather data from a lot of different sources and it sometimes isn't accurate.**

Something to note here...notice how we have not used the words "feel" and "felt" so far in this example. You can use those words, but I opted not to because it doesn't sound natural to me. I point this out because I think it's important to make things your own so you can speak as confidently and naturally as possible.

Found

The next portion of our FFFF is the one that causes the most problems for people. This is because it is easy to turn this part of the conversation into a sales pitch. That is not what you want to do at all, because you will come across as pushy. You want to explain how this person was in the same situation as the prospect and what actions they took to solve the problem. Here's an example.

> SDR: **What they found was that once they had all their data accurate and in one place, discovering the cause was pretty simple, and then, they were able to move on to solving it.**

Follow-up

The final part of our framework is the follow-up. This is simply asking a question to either book a meeting or to keep the conversation going. You will be customizing this often because the FFFF is a technique that can be used in a variety of situations. Here is an example of using it to ask for the meeting.

> SDR: **That being said, do you have 15 minutes to walk through how we've helped other companies organize and improve the accuracy of their data? How about tomorrow at 2?**

Take a look how this example comes together.

> SDR: **I know how painful that can be. A lot of marketing directors I speak with share the same frustration. They need to find the cause of a problem and, in order to figure it out, they have to gather data from a lot of different sources and it sometimes isn't accurate. What they found is that once they have all their data accurate and in one place, finding the cause is pretty simple. Then they can move on to solving it. With that said, do you have 15 minutes to walk through how we have helped other companies organize and improve the accuracy of their data? How about tomorrow at 2?**

There it is...the **FFFF** in action, and it has so many applications. Another way you can use this framework is to transition away from a topic that doesn't seem to resonate with the prospect. Let's take a look at an example of that.

> SDR: **I see what you're saying; that makes a lot of sense. Typically, when I speak with marketing directors who do not have a data collection problem, they tend to be focused on increasing the ROI of marketing spend. I'm curious, what is your current process for evaluating the ROI on your different inbound channels?**

With this framework we are able to build credibility while transitioning to another topic that the prospect may need some help with. This is the power of the FFFF—building credibility and relating to the prospect. Write down and practice your own feel, felt, found, follow-up that you can use next time you are speaking with a prospect.

The takeaway

The final technique I'm going to teach you is called the takeaway. I recommend that you use this after every one of the meetings you book. The goal of the take-away is to increase your meeting show-up rate by getting the prospect to recom-mit to the meeting that they just booked with you. Take a look at an example.

SDR: **Ok, Terry, I've scheduled 15 minutes for you to speak with Kelly on Wednesday at 2pm. Before I let you go, I want to make sure that this is going to be the best time for you. If not, we can cancel this now and pick a better one. Is this time best?**

As you can see, the takeaway starts off by repeating the time and date that the prospect agreed to. Directly after that we mention that we want to be sure that this time will be best for them, even though they just chose that time. Before let-ting them respond to that statement, we ask a question, "*If not, we can cancel this now and pick a better one. Is this time best?*" This question is very important and I would suggest that you do not change it. This is because we are using the word "cancel" which implies that it has already been scheduled. People do not want to cancel the meetings that they have committed to, but will decide not to show up to a sales call. By using this language we are making this meeting more important in the mind of the prospect.

Some SDRs have trouble using the takeaway, because they are nervous that the prospect will take them up on their offer and cancel the meeting. Do not be concerned about this for two reasons. First, if they agreed to a meeting with you, they most likely see the value and intend to show up. Second, if they do decide to cancel the meeting after the takeaway, then odds are they weren't going to show up in the first place.

CONCLUSION

You made it! We've covered a lot of information in this chapter and I know your mind must be spinning. Don't feel overwhelmed; take this information and im-plement it in pieces. Don't try and attempt every technique in this chapter on the phone tomorrow. Pick one, master it, move on to the next. Your goal is to become a great prospector, but you don't have to do that by the end of this week. Listen to your call recordings, focus on areas that you need to improve, then repeat. Stay disciplined and one day you will wake up and realize how much better you are now than when you started. Ok, let's move onto the next chapter.

STORY TELLING AND
THE ART OF CAPTIVATION

Back in the old days, towns would have large fire pits, where people would sit around and listen to the local storyteller. There were grand stories of giants, dragons, and epic battles; *Game of Thrones* has nothing on these guys! Times were simple back then and stories captivated the minds of many.

As humans, we love stories. It takes away from our daily life and allows our mind to let go of the stresses of life.

Between television, social media, and books, we are surrounded by stories all the time. We have more access than we've ever had in history. Can you imagine the storyteller at the town firepit holding an iPad? So much of life revolves around stories, I would even argue that a big part of living life is the creation of stories. This doesn't mean that everyone has the gift.

Many people are overwhelmed by the idea of telling a story because they don't feel they have anything interesting to say. This is far from the truth. Everyone has a story that they can tell, but they just don't know what it is yet. In most cases they simply lack story-telling confidence and their ability to deliver it in an interesting way.

Stories don't have to be about something extraordinary. Here's an example from when I was an SDR. I had a decision maker on the phone who told me that she couldn't speak because she was leaving for Italy in a few days. Before she hung up I asked if she had ever been there before. She hadn't. I launched into a story about a trip I took to Rome and caught someone trying to pickpocket me on a bus. The guy I caught was "the world's greatest pickpocket" according to an old Italian man standing across from me. I'm not sure how good a pickpocket you are if people know you as a pickpocket.

Does my story about a pickpocket in Rome have anything to do with the marketing software I was trying to sell? Absolutely not, and it's not even that great a story. I literally caught a guy with his hand in my pocket—I didn't discover

Hogwarts. The prospect I was speaking to got excited and we spoke for another five minutes about the trip she had planned. The simple story I told ignited our conversation and I was able to book a meeting with her for after she got back from Italy.

Stories are about building connections, rapport, and trust. Stories are arguably the most powerful tool you have in your belt for booking meetings, but it's a tool very few people know how to use.

THREE TYPES OF SELLING STORIES

Telling a story on a cold call isn't always relevant. Because of that it can be difficult to know when it's appropriate. In order to tell a story you must make sure that you've earned enough of your prospects time to tell it. Your story will not be effective if you get cut off halfway through with an "I'm too busy for this."

There's another important factor—the type of story you would like to tell; i.e. what are you trying to accomplish? There are three types of stories that come up on a cold call. Each type applies to a specific result you're trying to achieve. The three story types are social stories, solution stories, and pain stories. Each of these has a time and a place, so let's go through them one by one. While you read about each different type, write down a few ideas that you think might make a good story to use on your calls. We will talk story construction later on in this chapter.

SOCIAL STORIES

A social story is used when you're trying to build rapport with the prospect. This should be a story that is either funny or interesting. A social story can be built from something a prospect or client tells you or even your own personal experience. Remember the example I gave about my trip to Rome? I told that story with the specific purpose of building rapport with the prospect and it's a great example of a social story. The important thing to remember about a social story is that it must relate to what you are talking about and should be entertaining or interesting to the prospect. You do not want your prospect wondering why you are telling them this story halfway through.

SOLUTION STORIES

Often, when we're on the phone, we want to start talking about our product or service and how wonderful it is and how its specific features are going to help out the prospect. You and every other cold caller has the desire to do this and you better believe that your prospect has been through this song and dance before. A solution story is a great way to illustrate the results of your product or service without going into a full sales pitch.

The goal of a solution story should be to illustrate to your prospect the impact that solving their problem has. Do not pitch your product or service here. You will be building interest by association. The prospect will understand the benefits of your product or service and it will come across as more natural instead of being pushy and pitching your product or service.

PAIN STORIES

Pain stories are probably the least-used story type of the three. You may find yourself in the position of having to use an example of someone failing to solve a problem. This would come up if your prospect doesn't think that their problem is a big deal. A story we can tell to this type of prospect would give them an example of what happened to someone who didn't solve the main concern that the prospect also has.

Failure is a powerful motivator and using it to our advantage can be very useful. Careful story construction is necessary because you do not want to come across as negative. You do not want your story to shame the prospect by directly comparing what they are doing to someone else who has failed. You want to use a pain story as a way to <u>agree</u> with what the prospect is saying while giving an example that confirms their point.

CONSTRUCTING A STORY

The first thing you need to know about constructing a story is there has to be an actual point to telling it. You don't want to tell a story if there isn't a point to make. It is supposed to help you book a meeting.

The ability to create compelling stories takes a lot of practice and can be complex at times. Lucky for us, we aren't trying to write a novel. Well, I guess I am writing a book, but your goal is to engage with your prospects.

There is a basic structure of a good selling story—characters, situation, problem, solution, question. Let's take a look at each part.

- **Characters** - Who are the characters of your story?
- **Situation** - What is going on with the characters?
- **Problem** - What is the problem that your characters face?
- **Solution** - How do your characters solve this problem?
- **Question** - Follow up with a question to keep the conversation going.

The reason why a selling story can be effective is because it captures the attention of the prospect and gets them to forget they are on a cold call. Selling stories are great for making a point that can help you persuade the prospect later on in the call when you are asking for time on their calendar. In order to accomplish this we must follow the structure above to make sure that we hit all the components that go into a story. Let's walk through an example of a story built using this structure.

CHARACTERS

"It's funny you brought that up. Last week I was speaking with one of our long time clients. She's been the director of customer support for 30 years at ABC company and trust me, she will make sure you know about it."

SITUATION

"She was telling me how things used to be early in her career. Her team consisted of 30 customer support reps. It was her first time in management and she felt a little over her head."

PROBLEM

"One of the issues that kept coming up for her was that the customer support reps would not update all of the information that they were supposed to when completing a ticket. She kept reminding them but they still forgot."

SOLUTION

"She came up with a simple idea that she was very excited about. She went to Kinkos and had a checklist printed for every rep, detailing each step required when completing a ticket. She had the list laminated. I guess that was the thing to do back then. Anyway, she put the checklist on the desk of every one of her reps and that solved most of the problem. She told me the reps were forgetting to input the data because they didn't have a process for completing a ticket. What I learned from her is that simple ideas can have a huge impact."

QUESTION
"Anyway, I thought her story was great. I'm curious about your process though. What have you tried to get your reps to input data into the system?"

As you can see, this story is on the longer side and this is on purpose. If you are looking to tell a short story than take a look at the FFFF we covered in the previous chapter. The purpose of a longer story is to make a point. For example, the story in the example above is making the point that simple ideas can have a huge impact. This point is relevant because our goal is to book a meeting where we show the prospect our product or service, a product or service that is simple and makes a huge impact. Here are a few tips on how to create better stories.

Tip #1: Your story should relate to your prospect
If it doesn't, they won't listen to a word you're saying. The first part needs to get the prospect to visualize themselves as the person in the story. Of course, relating to the prospect's situation is the broader concept that applies to your entire story as a whole. The reason why we want to start our story off with something that is relatable is because we want to grab the prospect's attention and get them to listen.

Tip #2: Your story should draw a comparison
The comparison should be between your prospect and another person who overcame the situation that your prospect is in. It is very common to feel like problems are unique when that is typically not the case. Making a comparison is a great way to show the prospect that they are not alone and that there is a solution to their problem.

Tip #3: Your story should illustrate the solution to the problem.
When telling a story about someone who overcame a challenge, it's important to explain how they were able to do it. This does not mean you should start pitching your product or service. It's not the time or the place for that. Simply explain how they were able to overcome the challenge and, when it's time to talk about your product or service, a connection can be made.

FINDING INSPIRATION FOR YOUR STORY

Now, before you buy a funny hat, quit your job, move to the woods, and become an author, you should probably know how to find creative inspiration. This is the fun part and you have a lot of options for how you go about this.

THE CASE STUDY

The first thing you can do is adapt a case study that your company already has. A case study is a detailed example of a company's before and after using your product or service. If you don't have access to any case studies, you will have to create one yourself or try a different method for inspiration.

STORIES FROM OTHER SALESPEOPLE

Another way to find inspiration is speak with some of the salespeople at your company. Ask if they've heard any good stories from clients or have any good before and after examples to share. This can serve as a great way to learn about the impact your product or service has, as well as hopefully inspiring you to write a great selling story.

PERSONAL EXPERIENCES

You can always use your own experiences. This often creates the best selling stories. Don't worry, you don't even have to be that interesting to make it work! Your natural instinct might be to ask yourself "What interesting stories do I have?" Odds are you will come up blank.

What I recommend is choosing a specific time in your life and start from there. For example, ask yourself what you were doing when you were 20. Put yourself back in the shoes of a 25 year old you and take a look at what was going on then. What did you do for work? What did you do for fun? Who did you hang out with? What else did you do? Repeat this for different times in your life and see what memories pop up.

Just remember to snap out of it at some point, because we need you back on the phones.

STORY PRESENTATION

Constructing a compelling story is only half of the battle. You need to be able to tell that story to the prospect in a way that captivates them. At first, you may have a bit of a challenge with this; telling a story over the phone can be difficult. As you get more comfortable speaking over the phone, your ability to tell stories will improve as well. Over the phone, your tone of voice will play a huge role in how captivating your story is. The prospect cannot see your body language, so all they have to go on is your tone, word choice, and energy. This is like those old radio programs before the world had television—they used voice to paint the picture.

TONE

The tone of your voice always has a huge impact on how you are perceived on a call. Bring storytelling into the mix and it just adds to the importance. Vocal tone is a tool you must use to build credibility, rapport, and trust. When you are early in your sales career, you may find yourself sounding like a robot. This is because you are reading from a script and trying not to mess anything up.

If you want to improve your tone you need to do two things. First, listen to your own call recordings and then, listen to the call recordings of a person you believe has a great tone of voice. What differences do you notice? The person you would like to model your tone of voice after speaks deliberately. They are comfortable with pauses and they speak with a high level of confidence. Below are a few tips I've found to be helpful for people looking to improve their tone.

Tip #1: Control your rate of speech.
Most tone issues come from someone speaking too quickly because of nerves or excitement. Be very conscious of your rate of speech and slow yourself down, if necessary. Speaking too fast will give the prospect the impression that you lack confidence and aren't worth speaking with. Write the word "SLOW" on a sticky note and put it on your computer monitor. Whenever you see it while on the phone with a prospect, let it remind you to control your rate of speech.

Tip #2: Avoid the end of sentence uptone.
This typically happens at the very end of asking a question. During the last few words of that question your pitch may increase, getting higher and higher. This hurts your credibility because it will seem like you lack confidence

and that you don't know what you're talking about. To break this habit, practice asking questions while maintaining a strong, level tone of voice.

WORD CHOICE

The words you choose have a direct impact on the prospect's perception of you. Your word choice should change based on who you are speaking to. Have you ever noticed that you start using the same words and phrases as the friends you hang out with the most? By choosing words that your prospect has used or that you feel fit their personality, you can build rapport quicker. You will also be able to keep the prospect engaged in your story because you are speaking in a way that resonates with them.

When in conversation, try and pick up on words and phrases that your prospect uses often and write them down. For example, if the prospect you're speaking with uses the word "wonderful" whenever they talk about something they like, you have an opportunity to alter your word choice to match theirs. For instance you might want to say "The *cool* thing about automating your client follow up is…" If you alter your word choice to fit the prospect you may say "The *wonderful* thing about automating your client follow up is…"

When you tell a story make sure your word choices fit with the person you are speaking with. You may be able to use words or phases you've heard used earlier in the call. If you are unable to pick up on any unique words or phrases, use what you feel will resonate with the prospect. This takes practice, but once you get the hang of it you'll be able to build rapport faster.

ENERGY

When telling a story you have to stay engaged and keep your energy level high. It's very easy to sound scripted while telling a story. Energy is a tough subject to write about because it's something that you hear and feel. Think of all of the best storytellers you've listened to. Think of the way they enunciate their words, how they pause, what they emphasize. All these things come together to give them an energy you find compelling.

This isn't to say that you should try and mimic the style of a great story teller. You need to have your own correct energy for the story that you are telling. Just remember how they do it and apply your own personality to the story you tell.

If you're talking about a failing business that was able to turn things around, you should start with somber energy. Once the story becomes more positive, your energy needs to pick up as well. Movies use music to make us feel the way they want us to at that moment. Watch The Grudge without turning on the sound and the movie will just be about some lady with long hair. We can't play music during a call, or at least I have never tried. For our energy to captivate the prospect we must be just as invested in our story as we would like them to be.

CREATING YOUR COLD CALL CHARACTER

One of the most powerful stories that you have is your own. Unfortunately, you won't have the opportunity to tell this story to your prospects because they don't have all day! This comes across over the phone by how you communicate, I call this your cold call character.

Your cold call character is an "on phone" personality that prospects recognize you as. This is what they visualize when they hear your voice. If Mark Cuban gave you a call would you hang up on him? Probably not, because he has a personality that transcends a cold call. This is what we will create in this section. The goal is for you to walk away with a vision for how you want to be perceived over the phone. Then, it is your job to execute.

Creating your cold call character is broken down into four parts: attitude, character, backstory, and experiences. Attitude is how you come across on the phone. Character is who you are as a person. Backstory is why you are the way that you are. Finally, experiences are the actual events that got you there.

ATTITUDE

When creating your cold call character you must consider what your attitude is and how you respond to people responding to you. The reason why it is important to define this is because it will dictate how you come across in all situations, even ones that are unexpected. If you do not have your attitude defined, then it will change throughout a call. This has a negative impact on the person you are speaking with because you aren't consistent. Answer this question… using one word, how do you respond when someone asks you a question? Possible answers may be: thoughtfully, helpfully, informatively, curiously, confidently, energetically. What you may find is that you want more than one of these. This is normal, but for now, you must pick the one trait that is the most dominant. For our example, let's choose confident.

Using one word, how do you respond when someone asks you a question?

Confidently!

CHARACTER

Being clear about who you are as a person is a key element necessary for having presence over the phone. <u>You</u> know who you are as a person, but your prospect doesn't. Most people don't constantly represent who they really are and this is because we are so used to surface-level dialogue. Surface-level dialogue works great when you're ordering coffee or asking a coworker how their weekend was. When you're speaking with a prospect over the phone and want them to see you as someone who is high value, you must present yourself as such.

Answer these questions:

> **Question:** What does your character sound like?
>
> **Example answers:** Knowledgeable, energetic, calm, thoughtful, intelligent, confident, an expert.
>
> **Question:** How does your character build credibility?
>
> **Example answers:** Controlling the call, asking insightful questions, telling relatable stories.
>
> **Question:** What value do you bring to the prospect?
>
> **Example answers:** Industry expertise, infectious personality, innovative ideas. Below are the answers for our example character profile.

How You Might Answer These Questions

> **Question:** What does your character sound like?
>
> **Your Answer:** *An energetic problem solver.*
>
> **Question:** How does your character build credibility?
>
> **Your Answer:** *By referencing other customers who have experienced similar problems.*
>
> **Question:** What value do you bring to the prospect?
>
> **Your Answer:** *Creative thinking backed up by industry expertise.*

BACKSTORY

The backstory is the most fun part about building your cold call character. The reason why is because you get put together a character version of yourself. The backstory that you create doesn't have to be a mirror image of your own. You should have some fun with the story and ham it up a bit to make it memorable. Create a paragraph backstory following this structure. Where does your character come from, how do they view the world, what are they like when no one is looking, and what do they believe happiness is? Check out the example for our character profile.

My character is a good old southern boy who lives in the moment and is quick on his feet. He views the world like a giant playground and is excited to overcome any challenge that is thrown his way. He is passionate and positive even when no one is looking, he wears his heart on his sleeve. Happiness is spending time with people, laughing, and talking about life.

EXPERIENCES

The final step is collecting experiences that make you… well, you. These come in two forms. The first is knowing your life "path" and the second is having a few go-to stories to tell in different situations. Know your life "path" is another way of describing what your character has done. In our example character profile we might say something like this…

Character path story: My character grew up around a lot of family and had a very close relationship with them. He went to school with his siblings and cousins and there were social events every weekend. After high school my character went off to college and didn't have any family around. He had to rebuild this family structure with new friendships, which he did. This experience gave him the ability to build relationships quickly. He has the same mentality when it comes to selling—family first.

The second part is having some go-to stories that you can actually tell to prospects over the phone—stories that fit with your character. Take a look at the next example.

Stories to tell prospects example: I've been to Michigan before, with my family. We camped there by a lake and I'll never forget how beautiful it was, watching the sunset on the water while telling funny stories around the campfire. Have you ever camped there?

Here is our example character profile fully built out.

Using one word, how do you respond when someone asks you a question?

Confidently

What does your character sound like?

An energetic problem solver.

How does your character build credibility?

By referencing other customers who experienced similar problems.

What value do you bring to the prospect?

Creative thinking backed up by industry expertise.

Character path story: My character grew up around a lot of family and had a very close relationship with them. He went to school with his siblings and cousins and there were social events every weekend. After high school my character went off to college and didn't have any family nearby. He had to rebuild the family structure with new friendships, which he did. This experience gave him the ability to build relationships quickly. He has the same mentality when it comes to selling—family first.

Stories to tell prospects: I've been to Michigan with my family. We camped out by the lake and I'll never forget how beautiful it was, watching the sunset on the water while telling funny stories of the campfire. Have you ever camped there?

This is a very simple exercise and it may seem a little silly, but it's a lot of fun, especially in a group. It's fun to write down the character that you present over the phone, but more importantly, it gives you clarity. clarity on how you should come across on the phone will help you stay consistent.

Oh, and don't forget—this is the best part… Give your character a name. The one above we will call Good Old Boy Luke.

CONCLUSION

Telling a story can help create a connection that is vital to building strong rapport with the prospect. Storytelling comes naturally to some people, but many will need to spend time to improve in this area. Keeping a journal and writing down anything that happens to you that you feel would be a great story is important. Write often and practice story construction. You might even consider joining some public speaking groups or practice presenting your stories to friends and family.

As with most aspects of cold calling,
the more you practice the better you get.

OVERCOMING OBJECTIONS

Why do some people seem natural when it comes to selling, while others struggle to pick up the phone? No one is born with the ability to persuade; much of that skill is developed over time through life experiences and your relationship with rejection. The fear of rejection is very crippling and many people struggle with it. This manifests when they try and speak in front of a crowd, approach someone in public, or even when they need to pick up the phone and make a call. I have seen it time and time again—a sales development rep fails because they cannot handle the continuous rejection they get over the phone every day.

Rejection that stings the most comes in the form of an objection from the prospect. Different from the brush-off, the objection typically is near the end of the call when you're asking for the meeting. The reason this stings so much is because of all the work put in on the phone to get to the point of asking for the meeting, only to be turned down. This fear of rejection can keep the salesperson from asking for a meeting. You should never be afraid to ask for a meeting, to ask for the opportunity to show the prospect a solution to their problem. But, after facing rejection on a daily basis, some salespeople are.

YOU AREN'T ALONE

Every salesperson in every industry has come across an objection at one point or another. It's baked into the role of being a salesperson. Prospects will have objections. They may say they're too busy, or they don't have the budget, or they don't think you can help. It doesn't matter how you slice it, the prospect is telling you no and it's up to you to turn that into a yes. SDRs are lucky because they are only asking for the prospect's time, not their money. A prospect is more likely to give you 15 minutes of their time than a $2000 startup fee, $250 a month, and a year contract.

This doesn't mean that the objections on a cold call have less impact. An objection is an objection; it's a barrier to booking a meeting or closing a sale.

The focus of this chapter is on the objections that you will encounter on a cold call. In this chapter, we will cover the main causes of these objections and how to overcome them. This will serve as the foundation for overcoming more challenging objections as you progress in your sales career. Let's jump in and take a look at some reasons why an objection would be raised when trying to book a meeting.

REASONS FOR OBJECTIONS

✓ The prospect doesn't see the value in your product or service
✓ The prospect doesn't like you
✓ The prospect is afraid of change
✓ The prospect isn't ready to have this conversation now

In the vast majority of situations, the prospect is giving you an objection because they made a buying decision too early in the sales process. What do I mean by this? Typically, as an SDR, you want to build some interest and book a meeting for the prospect to speak with the salesperson whose job it is to motivate the them to make a buying decision. If the prospect makes a buying decision on the cold call, we have a problem on our hands. This is because they haven't seen our product or service yet and as a result, they are lacking complete information. If the prospect makes a buying decision on the cold call, that would require them to make a lot of assumptions, many of which will most likely be wrong.

PREMATURE BUYING DECISIONS

If you are able to keep the prospect from making a buying decision on the cold call, you will dramatically reduce the number of objections you receive. Buying decisions are typically made because the prospect feels they know enough about your product or service to evaluate its impact. The part that can be challenging is the amount of information required to cause this and that varies between decision makers. Some prospects think they know exactly what your product or service is after your introduction; others need you to give them more information about "how it works." It's important, in both of these scenarios, that you are able to identify when the prospect is at risk of making a buying decision.

The Technical Question

The key indicator that a prospect is at risk of making a premature buying decision is if they ask technical questions. Asking questions can be a sign of interest which is why it's easy to get excited and give the prospect too much information. If you do, it may result in a premature buying decision by the prospect. Combat this by careful answers to their technical questions and avoid what is called info dumping.

The Info Dump

Info dumping is when a sales development rep dumps a ton of information on the prospect all at once, hoping they will understand how great the product or service is. This can happen after the prospect asks a question or before the rep asks for the meeting. It's a desperate attempt to persuade the prospect to say yes. It is unfortunate when this happens, because the information that the SDR is dumping on the prospect is giving them enough information about the product or service to make a premature buying decision and not enough to make an actual buying decision.

When the prospect asks you a question about your product or service, you should answer with a high-level response, but then follow up with a question to them. Avoid going into too much detail, leaving the prospect with more to be desired. This works well for a basic question that may be asked, but what if the question does require greater detail? If the question can't be answered with a high-level response, you should defer the answer to the next meeting. Here's an example of what that looks like.

> Prospect: **So, tell me, how exactly does your system know when to prompt my reps to input the data?**

> SDR: **That's a great question and it's a bit technical for me. We can set up a time to have our product expert, Michelle, walk you through it. I'm curious though...what's the current process for your reps to input data?**

As you can see from this example, we admit we can't answer the question and imply that there will be another meeting. At this point the SDR might feel the urge to try and book that meeting. Remember, to avoid objections, the prospect must believe that your product or service could be the solution to their problem. If they don't believe that yet, you shouldn't ask for the meeting, but follow up with a question that will keep the conversation moving forward.

Too Late?

That's how we prevent a premature buying decision from being made, but what if it's too late? An indicator that the prospect has already made a buying decision, that we must reverse, would be if their tone changes from conversational to un-interested. The second that you notice this you must figure out what caused this sudden shift. It may be linked to the info dumping we talked about earlier, or a selling story that did not resonate. It could even be something you said that irritated them. Whatever the cause you must figure it out quickly and begin trying to repair the call.

TAKE A STEP BACK

Admit that you're far from where you should be. Follow this up by taking the prospect back to a time in the call where the conversation was going much better. The goal is to reverse the premature buying decision they might have made. Once you bring them back to that earlier point, ask a relevant question to keep the call moving. This should feel a bit like a reset. Take a look at the next example.

> SDR: **Let me take a step back here, because I went on a bit of a tangent. Earlier you were talking about how your reps don't input data consistently. Can you tell me more about how you're tackling this problem?**

Another indicator that you need to reverse a buying decision made by the prospect is when they tell you (*Who would've thought?*). If the prospect interrupts you to say that, they don't think your product or service would be valuable for them, you may become confused. How could they know that without understanding exactly what the product or service is? This is your opportunity to learn more. Ask them why they believe that and this will pull the objection out of them. Here is an example.

> Prospect: **You know, I just don't think this would be helpful for us.**

> SDR: **I understand and thanks for the honesty. Typically, when someone tells me that it's because I haven't done a great job explaining what we do. Would you mind giving me some insight into why you feel that this wouldn't be helpful for you?**

In this scenario we lost the opportunity to avoid or reverse the buying decision from being made, so we must now tackle the objection head on. This is ok and there is no need to be upset that your prospect has an objection. At the very least, receiving an objection means that they were listening.

So how do we overcome objections?
Great question, reader...a very thoughtful one indeed!

OVERCOMING OBJECTIONS

In this section we are going to cover how to overcome objections in the context of a cold call. The vast majority of cold calls are made with the intention of booking a meeting, which means we are asking for someone's time. This is very different than a closing call where we ask for the prospect to spend money. Because the technique is similar, getting good at overcoming objections on the cold call will also help you when you're in a closing role.

UNDERSTANDING

The first step to overcome an objection is going to seem simple. You need to make sure you actually understand the objection. It's very easy to get nervous, over-think things, or make incorrect assumptions when the prospect starts to give you an objection and you end up not fully understanding what they're telling you. If you don't listen carefully to the prospect and fully understand their objection, you will have a very low chance of overcoming it. Conversely, by understanding the prospect's perspective, you will be able to respond to their objection in a way that is thoughtful. You will actually convince them to meet despite originally declining.

Sometimes you will need more context to get a deeper understanding of the objection. This requires asking questions and intently listening so you understand everything connected to the prospect's objection. Let's walk through a quick example to illustrate this.

Prospect: **I appreciate the call Kyle, but I just don't think your product will be able to help us.**

SDR: **I hear you and that's not a problem. I would love to get some feedback. Why don't you think this will help you?**

Prospect: **Well, we have a very old system in place and I know it's going to be a headache to change.**

BOOM! *That's the objection! Did you see that!?*

Sorry, I get excited about these things. Let's break this down so you fully understand what happened. The prospect gave us a classic objection *"I just don't think your product will be able to help us."* If we try to overcome that objection without knowing the context, we will most likely fail because we have no idea what we have to overcome. Never assume you know what the prospect means. Always have them elaborate. In the example above once the prospect elaborated, we learned it's not that they don't think our product would benefit them—its that they believe changing from their current system is so challenging that they would never be able to receive the benefits of our product. Now that's a lot easier of an objection to overcome. After understanding their objection it's time for us to respond, so let's continue with our example.

> Prospect: **Well, we have a very old system in place and I know it's going to be a headache to change from.**
>
> SDR: **Just so I understand…you see the value of moving to a new ticketing system, but you just don't think it will be worth it because of the amount of difficulty you'll experience trying to switch?**
>
> Prospect: **Yeah, I just know that it'll be a pain.**
>
> SDR: **I totally understand your concern. Some of these old systems make it incredibly hard to move away from. Why don't we do this… Let's set aside 20 minutes to show you how simple it would be to change systems. We can walk you through how it will help insure that your reps input all the data you need them to. So, you'll have a stronger understanding of the quality of support a new system is giving you. If at that point you still think the transition process will be too painful, we understand. Do you have time tomorrow at 11am?**

In this response to an objection, the sales development rep is making the ask very small…ie *Can I have 20 minutes?* Doing this is important because the prospect's objection was very premature—no one had asked the prospect to make a painful change. In the next part of this response the SDR reminds the prospect of the result of their product, the result that's desired. Finally, the rep takes the pressure of the meeting away by giving all the control over the next meeting to the prospect, "If at that point you still think the transition process will be too painful we understand." Finally, the rep is assumptive and gives a time, making the meeting request very simple to agree to.

This is just one of the many objections you may get over the phone. You are going to be surprised at some of the reasons people give you for not being able to take a meeting.

Let's take a look at some common objections.

- I'm not interested
- I'm too busy
- I don't want to change
- We don't have the budget
- We're already going through this process with a competitor

These are basic objections and will be expressed in many different ways. It's your job to ask questions to get to the core of the objection, like we did in the example earlier. Regardless of the objection that you receive, you must respond and, you **must respond well**. Part of having a good response to an objection is about what you say and it must be done with confidence, caring, and patience.

THE MOST IMPORTANT ELEMENTS OF OVERCOMING AN OBJECTION

CONFIDENCE

I know this is going to come across as repetitive, so bear with me. Confidence is one the most important traits you can possess when making cold calls. The more confident you sound, the higher your perceived value, and this applies to objection handling just like it does other aspects of the call.

The difference is, when you ask the prospect a question and you don't sound confident, it's hard to recover. When you respond to an objection with a lack of confidence, you don't get that opportunity. Practice overcoming objections with colleagues and really put the emphasis on sounding confident, because there is simply no room for error.

CARING

Confidence is great, but it's only one piece of what's required to effectively re-spond to an objection. You must also have a caring attitude. If you truly don't have the prospect's best interest at heart, you should not be selling, period. Empa-thy goes a long way and, if you aren't genuine, the prospect will know. Having a caring attitude means coming at the objection from the side of the prospect and not your own interests. That's what's going to make you look good. You must be in their corner fighting for their needs, even if you have some bias to the situation. A cold call has very little to do with you and a lot to do with the prospect. It's about their needs, <u>not</u> your commission.

PATIENCE

Finally, overcoming objections is about having patience. Not all objections make sense; not all prospects understand value right away. When you are overcoming an objection, you must have patience and be willing to work with the prospect. What this means is when they don't understand the value or you don't understand their objection, <u>don't get frustrated</u>. Get back into the conversation and ask the prospect more questions to get a better idea of their perspective. Don't try to rush the prospect into booking a meeting. Take your time and respect their needs; it will go a long way.

THE PROSPECT ISN'T READY TO HAVE THIS CONVERSATION

In the vast majority of cases you received an objection because the prospect made a premature buying decision. However, you will run into the situation where the prospect is not making a premature decision—they are pushing off the decision. The prospect is telling you that they aren't ready to have a conversation now. In my opinion this is hands down, the hardest objection to overcome and let me explain why.

When a prospect asks you to reach out to them at a future time, it feels good, great even. You didn't get rejected and that feeling is similar to the one you get when you book a meeting. The reason this is the hardest objection to overcome is because there is no way to know if reaching out in the future will lead to a scheduled meeting. The prospect could be lying, procrastinating, or genuinely interested in speaking to you in the future. Another thing you have to remember is that you don't know what the future holds. Is the prospect going to quit their job in six months, forgetting they asked for a call back? Will the company's initiatives shift and they no longer have a need for your product or service? Worse-case scenario is that you call back and they've already signed with your competitor.

If all that wasn't enough, there is another reason why this is the hardest objection to overcome—if you try to overcome the objection, you could risk coming across as pushy. This is probably the worst part because we spend so much time building rapport and trust with the decision maker. All that work will be thrown out the window if they feel like we are pushing them into making a decision before they're ready. The question is, how do we navigate this objection? It's reminiscent of Shakespeare's Hamlet…

> *"To be, or not to be, that is the question."*

TO PUSH, OR NOT TO PUSH, THAT IS <u>OUR</u> QUESTION

Pushing the prospect a little is not necessarily a bad thing; sometimes it's completely necessary. The challenge is identifying when you need to push and when you should agree to call back at a later time. Always start with evaluating the quality of conversation, because this is the best indicator we have. If the call went amazingly, you had wonderful rapport, and the prospect is giving you a good reason why they need you to call back in a few months, you should respect that request. If the prospect doesn't have a reason to push the meeting off and they are experiencing a problem that they admit needing to solve, you should respectfully push them to take the meeting sooner.

THE SOFT PUSH

Let's take a look at an example of a an SDR respectfully pushing a prospect to take the meeting instead of putting it off.

Prospect: **Why don't we talk in 6 months?**

SDR: **That sounds great. I can absolutely reach out in six months. I am curious though…why do you feel that 6 months from now will be a better time to chat?**

Prospect: **Because I'm not sure if we have the bandwidth to implement something new right now.**

SDR: **I see. Well, since you're not in a position to implement anything new now, why don't we do this. Let's just walk through how our system improves your customer success teams efficiency and what it takes to implement. That way you can determine if you even want**

us to call back in six months. Do you have twenty minutes this friday at 11am?

We are agreeing with the prospect and offering a way for them to gain more information before making the decision to have us call back. The truth is, we are not changing our ask; the next call is going to be the same as it was before we got the objection. The only difference is that we are framing the meeting in a way that makes it more palatable for this prospect. This is an example of a soft push, one that is intended to change the perceived level of commitment you're asking for. In this next example, I am going to show you how to push a little harder.

Prospect: **Why don't we talk in 6 months?**

SDR: **That sounds great. I can absolutely reach out in six months. I am curious…why do you feel that 6 months from now will be a better time to chat?**

Prospect: **Because I don't really want to look at this right now, I have some other stuff on my plate.**

SDR: **I hear you. Kevin. Can I ask you a question that might be a little direct?**

Prospect: **Sure.**

SDR: **Earlier you said that improving the efficiency of your salespeople is your number one priority because of the time they're wasting. And, that's costing your company sales. I'm just curious, why would want to put off solving that problem?**

Did your hands sweat just reading that question? Calling out a prospect like this can be tough, regardless of how long you have been in sales. You're challenging them to take action and stop procrastinating. This takes a lot of confidence. The question may cause the prospect to say *"You're right. Let's set something up for next week."* Or…they will give you another objection. Either way, you're in a better place than you would be if you agreed to call the prospect back in 6 months. Now, you might be worried "what if they get upset?" Keep in mind you got permission to ask the question, so they most likely won't. If they do get upset, just apologize and move on.

If asking why they are putting off solving a problem that they admitted was a top priority does result in upsetting the prospect, odds are they weren't going to book a meeting with you in six months either.

HOSTILE PROSPECTS

In some cases you will be dealing with a unique type of objection. These are the objections you can't overcome with a response like we covered earlier in this chapter. You may find yourself on the other end of the phone with a hostile prospect. A hostile personality is an objection you will need to overcome. The hostile prospect will be aggressive, rude, and try to bully you. The first time you speak with a hostile prospect you will have either one of two reflexes—fight or flight. You will either apologize profusely and end the call quickly or you will double down, lock horns, and battle it out. I love to battle it out as much as the next guy, but that is not the correct way to approach this and neither is apologizing and then ending the call.

WHY ARE THEY HOSTILE?
There are three reasons why a prospect might be hostile with you over the phone.

- They don't like cold calls
- You caught them at a very bad time
- They simply have a hostile personality.

Regardless of the reason, when you are confronted by a hostile prospect, the only way you will be able to turn the call around is by getting them out of their hostile mode. I have four tips on how to handle a hostile prospect.

Tip #1: Stay calm and keep your tone consistent.
When dealing with someone who has a high level of aggression, it's natural to increase your rate of speech and raise your tone. I recommend staying calm and not to waver in your confidence. This will show the prospect that you are not intimidated and will not be pushed around. "This is my lunch money!"

Tip #2: Do not get defensive.
Responding with a sharp or defensive tone will only exacerbate the problem and control that urge to fight back. A hostile prospect will feed off your energy so it's important to keep your cool and not attempt to match their energy.

Tip #3: Give them the illusion of control over the call.
When a hostile prospect is drilling you with questions, it's important not to dodge any, because this is what they're hoping to catch you doing. You should answer their question clearly and respond with a question of your own.

Tip #4: Find common ground.

Listen to what the prospect is saying and see if you can find something that will help you establish common ground. You're trying to find a window that will let you start to build a connection. Another great tool to find common ground and reduce tension is using your sense of humor.

Let's take a look at an example of how a call with a hostile prospect can play out when using these tips.

Prospect: **Look. I'm sick of getting calls like this all the time!**

SDR: **I hear you. You probably get bombarded by people trying to get you to make changes.**

Prospect: **Yes, and it's frustrating!**

SDR: **Totally! Look, your business is successful and if you have a good system over there I don't think you should change it. I'm curious…how are you keeping track of the deals your sales reps have in their pipeline?**

Prospect: **I have a spreadsheet that they're supposed to fill out. Wait, what do you guys do?**

SDR: **We help business owners keep track of the pipeline of their sales reps so they can forecast earnings more accurately. Most folks I speak with are focused on increasing the efficiency of their salespeople. Is that the same for you or are you more focused on getting accurate data reporting?**

As you can see in the example the SDR didn't have a magic sentence that defused the prospect. They focused on finding common ground with the prospect and asking questions to keep them talking. However, even doing this won't always win a hostile prospect over. You may have to use a technique that is near and dear to my heart—giving the prospect an out. Check out this example and then we'll go over why this is effective.

Prospect: **I have a lot of focuses right now! I am sick of these calls. You are scum!**

SDR: **Listen Frank, If I said something that upset you that was not my intention. If you'd like, I can end this call now or we can quickly see if this is something that would be valuable for your company.**

Can you guess why I love this technique so much? Confidence! That's right! It requires you to have high confidence! Let me explain why this is an effective way to defuse hostile prospects. The first sentence is designed to force the prospect to take a step back and notice how they're coming across. The clever phrasing of "If I have said something that offended you" is designed in a way to cause your prospect to realize that they have come across as hostile and are the ones responsible for your experience. This is followed up with confidently offering to end the call, something most salespeople would be too afraid to do. Giving the prospect an out is a technique that should only be used if you have exhausted your other options with no success.

CONCLUSION

Objections are going to happen, No one can avoid them. What will aid your success as a sales development rep and throughout your sales career is not letting an objection throw your confidence. Know that objections are coming and don't be caught off guard when they arrive. To be able to keep your confidence you must practice responding to objections often. Sales requires a lot of repetition, which is why salespeople typically get better over time. Of all the calls you make, only a small percent will be decision makers, which means you will not get the opportunity to overcome objections as often as you get the opportunity to speak with gatekeepers. Because of this, it's very easy to get rusty and lose meetings that you would have booked had you kept yourself sharp.

Practice, practice, practice.
It may never make you perfect, but
it sure will make you better!

EVERYTHING PROSPECTING
(FROM FIRST TOUCH
TO SHOWING UP TO THE MEETING)

At this point in the book I would imagine you have a lot of questions, questions that have been piling up throughout each chapter. *How do I do this? When should I do that? What should I do if this happens?* The list goes on and on, I'm sure. In this chapter I'm going to do my best to answer those questions, without even knowing what they are! We're going to go on a journey together, a journey into the world of prospecting. In this chapter we will start with a high-level look at the sequence of prospecting events. After that we're diving into detail about each of the prospecting methods available to us. Finally, our journey will end with what you are responsible for after you book a meeting.

THE JOURNEY OF AN ACCOUNT

I'd like to begin this chapter with a high-level overview of the journey an account takes. From the very first touch by the sales development rep, to the meeting taking place between the decision maker and the sales rep, there are a lot of potential twists and turns that can cause an account to take a different path than what you've planned. Keep in mind that things don't always go the way you want, so it's important to know what your plan is.

THE BEGINNING
All great journeys have a beginning and for an account this beginning is when it's discovered by a sales development rep. The SDR will add a contact from that account into his or her sequence. A sequence is a series of touch points utilizing

different methods of communication. We will go into detail about sequences later in this chapter. Here is a high level overview of the journey of an account.

- Throughout the contact's time in the SDR's sequence, they will receive phone calls, emails, maybe some snail-mail, and even a possible LinkedIn communication.

- At some point, the contact will respond to the SDR and agree to a meeting and that SDR will cry tears of joy and walk around the office telling all his colleagues.

- After an hour of frolicking, the SDR will send a calendar invite to the contact and finish the administrative work required after booking a meeting.

- Before the meeting takes place, the contact will receive a call and/or an email reminding them of the date and time of the meeting.

- Finally, the contact shows up to the meeting and it goes swimmingly!

- The salesperson is happy because they have a quality opportunity; the SDR is happy because they created that opportunity; the contact is happy because they've found a solution to a business problem they are facing.

This is the ideal scenario, but as I mentioned before, things don't always go smoothly. Throughout an account's journey there will be uncontrollable events that strike when least expected. Some of these events will be your responsibility to navigate, but there will be others where your efforts will have no impact. You must not dwell on the individual events that cause an account to take longer to progress through this journey than expected. If you get too focused on individual accounts, you will fail to see the big picture and that may result in missed opportunities. Fortunately, there is a way to ensure you never lose sight of that big picture, while continuing to focus on each individual account.

SEQUENCE

When prospecting, an SDR must utilize multiple methods of outreach to maximize their chance of a booked meeting. This means phone calls, emails, and LinkedIn activities. Each one of these methods has its own unique quirks and requires careful execution. The rep must strive to improve in every outreach method available to them and, if they do, it will lead to their success. The magic happens when these methods of prospect communication come together and are used in harmony—i.e. *this is your sequence.*

A sequence is a collection of touch points organized over a period of time. Another way to think about it is that it's the sequence of prospecting methods you use on each contact over a period of time. For example, if you have a contact at an account who you would like to make contact with, you would add that contact to a sequence. That sequence would instruct you to call the contact and then, a few days later, to send an email, and then, another call, followed by a LinkedIn message, etc. Take a look at this diagram.

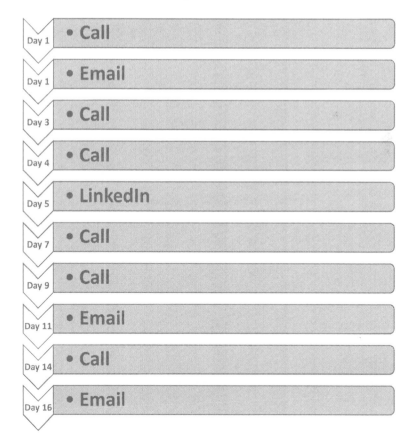

CREATING A SEQUENCE

The first thing worth mentioning is that typically, a sequence would be created with a sales enablement tool, such as Apollo.io, one of the leading sales engagement platforms, helping sales organizations deliver a better sales experience for their customers.

Organizing each account with multiple contacts associated with them, creating a sequence without a tool will most likely cause more problems than it's worth. I am going to continue this section under the assumption that you will be using a sales enablement tool.

SEQUENCE COMPONENTS

There are two main components of a sequence—day and step. When I mention *day,* I am referring to an actual day in the sequence—I am talking about *time*. If you have a contact on day three of your sequence, that would mean that you added them three days ago and presumably, have already attempted to make contact. When I mention *step,* I'm referring to what touchpoint they are scheduled to receive—I am talking about *action*. For example, that same contact on day three in your sequence may be on step 2. If this was the case it would indicate that your second attempt at contacting the prospect happens on day three.

Why is this important? Because we want to use multiple methods of communication, but at different frequencies and over different periods of time. The goal is to maximize our chance at getting in contact with a decision maker or stakeholder. The spacing between steps, what method we use for each step, and how those methods interact, have an impact on our ability to book a meeting. The follow up question you may be asking is...

"Ok, Kyle, what's the best sequence?"

Great question!!

Well, honestly, there is no best sequence. I know, that can be a tough pill to swallow. Sequences are as unique as fingerprints and what works best in some industries will not work as well for others. That being said, we can construct a sequence that will serve as a starting point. We can build a sequence using best practices that we see in other companies. There has been a lot of research on this topic so feel free to explore and create your own. For now, however, here's what I would suggest and why.

Following is a very simple 7x16 sequence—**7 touches over the course of 16 days.** The reason why I suggest starting with this sequence is because at the time of writing this there has been a lot of research published that says that 7 touches is optimal. You don't want to miss out on opportunities by not following up enough times. You also don't want to waste your time following up with prospects who will not respond. 7 touches seems to be the sweet spot. The amount of days that goes by is going to depend on the nature of your business. You may want to be more aggressive, or less so. That's up to you to decide, so this sequence is built somewhere between aggressive and periodic.

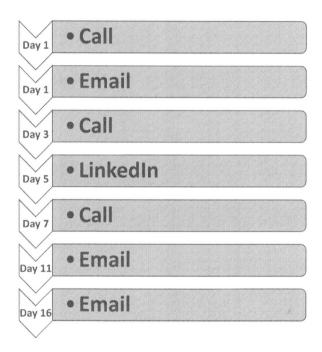

Day 1 • Call
Day 1 • Email
Day 3 • Call
Day 5 • LinkedIn
Day 7 • Call
Day 11 • Email
Day 16 • Email

HOW MANY SEQUENCES SHOULD YOU HAVE?

As you can imagine sequences can get out of hand rather quickly. It isn't uncommon for most of an SDR's sales enablement tool to be a graveyard of old sequences, with nothing left except some analytics to remember them by. Because experimenting with sequences is fun, it can also be a big distraction and that, I recommend you try to avoid. I do, however, see value in experimentation and don't want to discourage you to think outside the box.

Here's a simple rule that should help you avoid wasting time building too many sequences. Ask yourself "*What metric am I trying to improve and, if I am successful, what impact will that have?*" If you answer this question and the metric you are trying to improve has a sizable impact on productivity, go ahead and test out your sequence idea. If you cannot answer the question or the metric goal you are striving for doesn't have a significant enough impact, move on.

3 KEY SEQUENCES

There are three sequences that I believe every rep should have—a sequence for cold accounts, one for warm accounts, and one to reschedule meetings. If you have a sequence built for each of these situations, you will be well positioned to tackle the vast majority of situations. We've already covered a sequence for working cold accounts, so let's focus on warm accounts.

WARM ACCOUNTS SEQUENCE

When you speak with a contact for one of your accounts, they may ask you to reach back out to them in a few months. This could lead to a meeting, but the prospects request to reach back out is far enough away that we risk them forgetting about our conversation. Because we want to capitalize on our first conversation and stay relevant to the prospect, add them to a warm account sequence. The purpose of this sequence is to help the prospect remember the conversation where they asked you to reach back out in a few months and to provide them with some value in the form of resources and articles. You are staying connected with the prospect by periodically reaching out. Let's take a look at a simple warm accounts sequence.

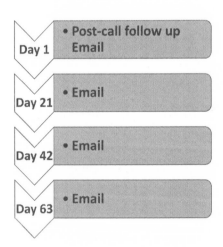

Day 1	• Post-call follow up Email
Day 21	• Email
Day 42	• Email
Day 63	• Email

Call with a follow-up email, then a **Step** every 3weeks.

This sequence begins the day that you had the call with the prospect and the first step is sending a post-call follow-up email. We will cover the content of an email like this later in this chapter. For now, notice the spacing between steps—three weeks. Every three weeks this sequence will prompt us to send a custom touchpoint. What touchpoint you send is your decision and should be relevant to your prospect. You are not reaching out every three weeks with the intention of booking a meeting. The goal is to reach out every three weeks and provide some value that will keep you top of mind with the prospect. A great example would be sending the prospect a blog post that you read that's relevant to their industry or any resource that you believe would be helpful for them. This is something that gives the prospect the impression that you are thoughtful and care about them beyond just booking a meeting. This aids you immensely when the time that the prospect asked you to reach out arrives and you call them to book a meeting. Here is an example of what that might look like being sent to a prospect in the artificial intelligence space.

Hi Bill,

I just finished reading [Link]this article that I thought you might enjoy. It's about a company in Georgia developing an A.I. that will be able to train a dog! Wow! How far away do you think we are from no more potty accidents in the house?

Best,

Kyle

RESCHEDULE MEETING SEQUENCE

Not all of your meetings are going to materialize. Yes, it's sad I know. In order to stay organized with your rescheduling efforts. you should build a reschedule meeting sequence. We will cover the messaging you should be using when attempting to reschedule a meeting in chapter 9. For now, let's take a look at what a reschedule meeting sequence looks like.

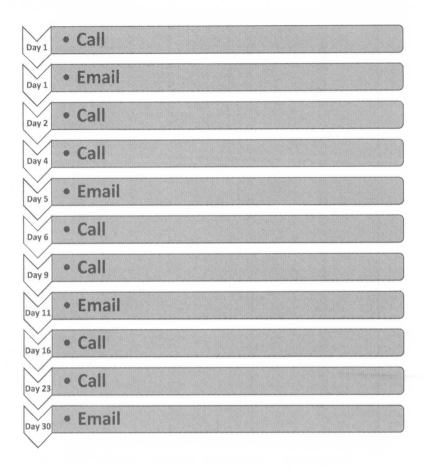

Call with a follow-up email, then a **Step** every few days.

As you can see, this sequence starts off with a lot of touchpoints very close together. This is because our best chance of rescheduling is shortly after the meeting was supposed to take place. You will also notice this sequence lasts a lot longer than our others have. Rescheduling a meeting is easier than booking it was, so it's worth extending the time we continue to make attempts to connect with the prospect.

Having a sequence for cold accounts, warm accounts, and one for rescheduling meetings will keep you organized in the vast majority of situations. Organization is important to ensure that things aren't slipping through the cracks.

If you haven't thought of this next question yet, you will at some point…

What do we do when we have multiple
contacts at an account?

WORKING MULTIPLE CONTACTS

Having multiple contacts at an account is necessary in many situations, but it also complicates your processes. "What do I do if...?" Questions pop up frequently. The answers aren't always intuitive. So, how do you properly work more than one contact at an account? How do you handle some of the common situations that come up?

Let's begin with when you should add a second contact to a sequence.

ADDING ANOTHER CONTACT

Adding a second contact at one of your accounts to your sequence will increase your chances of connecting with someone from that account. This is a huge up-side that is absolutely worth your time, but, there are also downsides to consider.

The first contact we add to our sequence will typically be the main decision maker. That means that every contact we add, after the first, is getting farther and farther away from the decision maker. For the most part this is not great because ideally, our meetings are booked with people who have decision-making authority. This is not always the case. Booking a meeting with a stakeholder in the decision-making process can be an effective entry point into an account. It is up to you and your company to decide who you should be meeting with.

As I mentioned earlier, the main value of adding the second contact is to increase our odds of connecting with someone at the account. If we were to add the first and second contact to our sequence at the same time, we would spend twice the amount of time working one account, because we would be reaching out to both contacts. If the decision maker answers the phone on the second call we make, it wasn't necessary to add that second contact. This is why I recommend adding the second contact *after three touches* to the first contact without any response. I would even recommend adding it as a step in your sequence, so you won't forget.

BREAKING THE RULES OF THE SEQUENCE

HAVE TO? WANT TO? NEED TO?

Sometimes it's necessary to break some rules, which I love to do. There are three different scenarios for when you will need to break away from the safe structure of your sequence—when you have to, when you want to, and when you need to.

Have to?

You will **have to** break away from your sequence whenever your prospect has engaged in some way with your messaging. For example, your sales enablement tool alerts you that your prospect is reading your emails. If this happens you will engage in something I call "***speed to lead***." I didn't make the term up, but I love it. Speed to lead is when a prospect engages with your messaging and you give them a call as fast as possible. Research shows that if you call a prospect quickly after they engage, you have a dramatically higher chance to connect.

Want to?

You will encounter times when you will **want to** break away from the shackles of sequence structure (next book title?). You will get this urge when you want to test some different messaging or try out a new prospecting tool, like adding a video to your email. I encourage you to experiment and go against the grain from time to time. When you do this, choose what metrics you are tracking and decide what success will look like. Like I explained in a previous chapter, it is important when you're testing something to know what metric you are trying to improve and what the impact of succeeding will have. As long as you are clear about that, test away, my friend.

Need to?

The final situation that will cause you to put on a bandanna and break the rules is when you **need to**. You may find yourself in a position where you're on the cusp of hitting quota and need one or two more meetings. In this situation you will need to break the sequence rules and engage in my favorite prospecting activity—**dialing!** One of the main reasons why I think the phone is the most powerful prospecting tool is because it has the ability to move the needle quickly. If a prospect reads an email you sent, they may eventually respond to it. If you get the prospect on the phone, they will immediately respond to you, positive or negative. Whenever you are in a position where you need to move the needle, *quickly, simply...smile and dial.*

EMAIL

Using email to book meetings can be a challenge, because of the number of emails prospects get and how easy those emails are to ignore. You have to stand out in an environment where everyone is trying to stand out. Do you think a peacock would catch your eye if you were at Coachella music festival? This characteristic can cause SDRs to spend way too much time customizing emails, only to have them end up in the trash.

In this section let's cover how to write an engaging email tailored to your prospect and what you should automate to increase your efficiency. Before we dive into the writing, let's talk about how to research the information that you can use in those emails

THE 3X3 RESEARCH METHOD

There is a popular research method called 3x3 research. The basic premise is to find three pieces of information about the contact you are targeting in three minutes. Three minutes isn't much time so don't feel bummed if your research is taking a bit longer. What you will find is that the more contacts you have researched in your career, the quicker you are able to find useful information. This is because you will know what to look for and where to look.

What you are looking for is any useful information that you can use to build rapport with the prospect by showing that you did your research and are thoughtfully reaching out. Now, before you start digging through LinkedIn pages and crossing your fingers in hopes that you went to the same college as one of your prospects, remember what I said earlier. Everyone is trying to stand out. So, when they zig you have to zag.

A college connection is good, but don't stop there. Take a look at a list of potentially useful information that you may be able to find online about one of your prospects.

- You both went to the same college
- Similar hobbies and interests
- You have read their favorite book and can quote it
- Similar career path
- Their profile picture is at a location that you've been to
- They created a piece of content you can reference
- Their company was in the news for something exciting
- You're in the same group on LinkedIn
- Interesting piece of industry-related news
- Industry-related content

This list has a few examples of what you might be able to find when doing 3x3 research. When choosing the research you are looking for, make information about the individual contact a priority. Tailoring your emails with information that is relevant to the contact will have the largest impact on their response rate. You may find yourself in a position where you can't find much about the individual contact and you'll have to venture out and research the company itself. When using company research to aid you in tailoring emails, try and find news or an interesting fact that you'll be able to relate to the contact. For example, if you are tailoring an email to the VP of sales and are able to find an article talking about how their company had a huge sales month you should use that because it's extremely relevant.

Three useful pieces of information in three minutes!

Time yourself and really make an effort to keep your research to under three minutes. Being able to tailor your emails to the prospect is powerful and will have an impact on your response rate. It can also be a time hog. If you're not careful you'll look at the clock and realize that you've been reading LinkedIn recommendations for twenty five minutes. To help keep your research in the three-minute timeframe, have a hit list of websites you will use and create a research workflow. Here is an example of a research workflow.

Organize your research workflow from your most effective research source to the least. By doing this, you will be able to finish your research faster, because time will not be used on less effective research methods (unless necessary). There are also tools that you can use to aid in your research and some are even built into the sales enablement tool you are already using. Do what you can to increase your efficiency, so you'll always be able to keep the research under three minutes.

TAILORING EMAILS

Once you have your research, you must now use it to tailor your emails to the prospect. We will talk about how to write a paragraph body later on, but for now,

I want to focus on the first few sentences in the email. This is where you'll be doing the bulk of your tailoring. First, let's use a piece of information as an example.

In our research we discovered that our contact wrote an article called "The 3 Big Mistakes Most Hiring Managers Make, and How to Avoid them." In the article our contact wrote about how most hiring managers start the process too late, which causes them to be desperate for talent. This leads to poor decision making during the interview process.

This is a great piece of information to use when tailoring our email. Other than the subject line, the most important part of our email is the first sentence. This is because most email service providers show a preview of the email and the first sentence is what is on display. Lead with something that grabs their attention and shows that the email is meant for them specifically. Let's take a look at an example.

Hi Jessica,

Your article about the mistakes hiring managers make was spot on!

When your prospect sees that the first sentence of your email relates to something they did, something they are proud of, they will feel compelled to open it. As the prospect is reading our email, we want to make it clear that we didn't just read the title. Let's be a little more thoughtful, see example below.

Hi Jessica,

Your article about the mistakes hiring managers make was spot on! I think another reason why most hiring managers start the process late is because in our startup culture, the decision to hire comes after realizing a need for a specific role and, of course, they needed it yesterday. Any plans on writing an article about how to better forecast hiring needs?

The information we found in our research came together to create a very strong introduction. We grabbed the prospects attention by showing that we read their article. After that we added our own take on what we read, showing that we actually read it. We follow up with a personal question that also serves as inspiration for the prospect's next article. This introduction is thoughtful and should do a good job of getting the attention of the prospect. Remember, this is the goal of tailoring an email. You can use the same framework to tailor an email with any information that you find in your research. Once you have created a strong, tailored introduction you will need to back it up with a compelling email body.

WRITING THE BODY OF AN EMAIL

The body of your email is intended to pique the interest of the prospect and ultimately get them to agree to have a quick call or book a meeting. Which outcome you strive for depends on the amount of qualifications you require before booking a meeting. I am going to assume you have an average amount of qualifications and will be trying to get the prospect to agree to a quick call with you.

The body of your email will be a template that you will use for the majority of your prospecting emails. There may be some light tailoring required but the main idea is to have an email body that you can "cut and paste" as many times as you need to. Check out this example.

In addition to liking your article I was reaching out because one challenge most hiring managers I speak with face is quality candidates withdrawing before the final interview.

We help fast-growing tech companies reduce the amount of days between interviews, resulting in a 30% decrease in time from application to offer and a 15% increase in successful hires. If this resonates, we should set up a quick call. Do you have some time tomorrow at 11am?

Best,

Kyle

The body of our email does a couple of things that all come together to motivate action. It starts off with explaining a challenge that the prospect is most likely experiencing. Being able to identify a prospect's challenge gives credibility. In the next paragraph of our email we explain the type of companies we help and the impact our product makes. We use numbers here because we want the prospect to visualize what impact having that result would have on their business. Finally, we end with an assumptive ask for time. Let's take a look at the entire email from tailored introduction.

Hi Jessica,

Your article about the mistakes hiring managers make was spot on! I think another reason why most hiring managers start the process late is because in our startup culture, the decision to hire comes after realizing a need for a specific role, and of course, they needed it yesterday. Any plans on writing an article about how to better forecast hiring needs?

In addition to liking your article. I was reaching out because one challenge most hiring managers I speak with face is quality candidates withdrawing before the final interview.

We help fast growing tech companies reduce the amount of days between interviews, resulting in a 30% decrease in time from application to offer and a 15% increase in successful hires. If this resonates, we should set up a quick call. Do you have some time tomorrow at 11am?

Best,

Kyle

This email is tailored to a specific person and should do a great job getting that person's attention. The next step for you is to create an email template so you can quickly populate the bulk of your email and just tailor what you need to. Let's take a look at what this would look like.

Hi {{first.name}},

{{Tailored introduction with research}}

I was reaching out because one challenge most {{title}} I speak with face is {{potential problem of the prospect}}.

We help {{industry}} {{solution to problem}} resulting in {{result}}. If this resonates we should set up a quick call. Do you have some time {{date and time}}?

Best,

{{my.first.name}}

Having a template built out will save you some time when constructing each email. You might have noticed we are missing one more piece that is very import-ant for an email. This is of course the subject line. If you do a quick google search for "sales email subject lines" you will be overwhelmed with the amount of email subject lines that boast "best open rates!" For this reason, I am not going to go into too much detail about email subject lines, but I want to give you just a few tips that I have found useful over the years.

Tip #1: Use your research when appropriate.

If you were able to find some interesting information through your research, you should leverage that in your subject line as well. In the example above, we discovered that the prospect had written an article. An appropriate subject line to use could be *"Your article about avoiding hiring mistakes"*.

Tip #2: Try using the prospect's name.

Using the prospects name can be an effective way to boost your open rate. When someone sees their name it draws their eye quickly, because it's so familiar. This coupled with a strong first sentence is a good recipe to get anyone to open an email.

Tip #3: Avoid hype.

I strongly recommend avoiding subject lines that comes across salesy or automated. For example "Increase your productivity 50%!" Always tailor the subject line to the person that you are sending the email to. For example *"Question about your recent round of funding"* or *"Ideas for improving your hiring process."*

OTHER SEQUENCE-RELATED EMAILS

Throughout a sequence you will be sending more than one type of email. You will be trying different techniques to get the prospect to respond. I have drilled down these emails into 4 different categories: reminder, second angle, wake up, and break up.

Reminder

The reminder is the simplest email you will send and perfect for automation. The goal of this email is to remind the prospect that we sent them an email in order to elicit a response. The response email should be a reply to the first email you sent, so your prospect doesn't have to go digging for it. Here is an example of a reminder email.

Good morning Jessica,

Did you get my last email by chance?

Second angle

Another email that you will be sending is what I call the second angle. This email is built using a different problem that your product or service solves. The problem you bring to the prospect's attention in the first email might not resonate with them. The second angle email gives us another shot at building some interest. Read the example below, and notice it fits our first emails structure.

Hi Jessica,

I sent you an email the other day and felt it was worth following up.

I speak with people who are responsible for the hiring process and they tell me they spend a lot of time reading resumes of candidates who aren't qualified.

We help fast growing tech companies use A.I. to screen resumes and make sure only qualified candidates make it through. This results in hours of freed-up time and quicker identification of the highest quality applicants. If this resonates, we should set up a quick call. Do you have some time tomorrow at 11am?

Wake up

Your contacts may get far through your sequence without you being able to connect with them. As they get closer to the end, we change our email strategy from trying to find a time to have a call to getting a response. This next email is called the wake up, because it's designed to "wake up" the prospect and get a response from them.

Hi Jessica,

I've made a few attempts to connect about helping with your recruiting efforts.

Is there someone else I should speak with or is now just a bad time?

Let me know either way so I can follow up accordingly.

Best,

Kyle

_____

Break up

The final email of your sequence is called the break up. This is our final attempt to get the prospect to respond. We have made multiple attempts to contact this prospect, from phone calls to LinkedIn; nothing was successful. So now it's time for a last-ditch effort. At this point you have a lot of flexibility with what you can try, so feel free to experiment. Below is an example that makes me laugh.

_____

Hi Jessica,

I've been reaching out for a few weeks now and have not received a response. When this happens it is usually for 1 of 3 reasons.

1. You are interested but are swamped and haven't been able to respond

2. You aren't interested and are hoping that I go away

3. A filing cabinet has fallen on you and you can't get up

If it's number 1 or 2, just respond back with the appropriate number and I will respond accordingly. If it's number 3... Should I call 911?

Best,

Kyle

_____

Post call email

The final email I want to cover in this chapter is the post call email. You will use this email if you've had a good conversation with a prospect, but they didn't schedule a meeting. The purpose of this email is to reinforce the positive interaction that you had and start to build a relationship that will help with future follow ups. Here's an example of a post call email.

Subject: It was a pleasure speaking with you

_____

Hi Jessica,

Thanks so much for your time on the phone today. I appreciate you filling me in about the challenge you're having keeping track of your most qualified candidates. You're not alone. This is a common problem for most companies growing at your speed.

Here is a [Link] blog post from a month ago that goes into detail about this issue. I look forward to reconnecting in January. Feel free to reach out to me directly if you have any questions.

Best,

Kyle _____

USING LINKEDIN

The effectiveness of LinkedIn is going to vary greatly based on industry, decision maker, and your product or service. How you plan to fit LinkedIn into your overall prospecting strategy is going to be a decision that you, or your company, will have to make. In this section we will cover my suggestion of where LinkedIn fits in your prospecting strategy and how to use it to engage with your prospects.

HOW LINKEDIN FITS IN YOUR PROSPECTING

There's a lot of debate around how SDRs should be leveraging social media in their prospecting efforts, specifically LinkedIn. Some say it should be your very first touch, while others suggest utilizing it as a backup tool when your other connection attempts have failed. I fall into the second camp in most situations and here's why. We've spoken a lot about time management in this book and at this point you should be sold on its importance. My opinion is that LinkedIn is not widely used enough in most industries to be worth using it as a first touch. To be clear, if you are selling into an industry where LinkedIn is actively used by most decision makers, then you will want to leverage this tool more.

SENDING LINKEDIN DIRECT MESSAGES

LinkedIn requires that you subscribe to their Sales Navigator product in order to send messages to people you aren't connected with. These messages will go wasted if sent to a prospect who doesn't have the LinkedIn app and who rarely checks the website. There are some industries where the opposite is true, for example, tech companies. If you are in an industry with heavy LinkedIn activity then use it early. If not, stick with a more traditional means of communication. Then, after the first three or four touches, leverage LinkedIn.

It is also important to mention that LinkedIn may temporarily ban your account if you send too many connection requests that have a low acceptance rate and you are not a Sales Navigator user. So, don't try to connect with every contact at every account that you find. Instead, send a connection request to the prospects that you've connected with as a way to stay in touch with them. This will increase your chances of being accepted as a connection and getting the opportunity to engage with your prospect via LinkedIn.

THE LINKEDIN MESSAGE

Writing emails and sending messages seem similar on the surface, but they vary deeply in application. Typically, you will be sending a message to a prospect through LinkedIn after attempting to connect with them via phone and email. Because of this, you shouldn't copy and paste the email and click send, because it will definitely have a negative impact. Use LinkedIn as a follow-up touchpoint, referencing our previous contact attempts, and offering our prospect an easier way to communicate. Let's take a look at an example related to our example email from the email section.

Good morning Jessica,

I sent you an email the other day with my thoughts regarding your recent article, great stuff! I'm messaging in case you prefer to communicate this way.

We help fast growing tech companies reduce the amount of days between interviews, resulting in a 30% decrease in time from application to offer and a 15% increase in successful hires. If this resonates, we should set up a quick call. Do you have some time tomorrow at 11am?

If there's a better contact, please feel free to send me their way.

Best,

Kyle

As you can see, this message is more casual, shorter, and gives them the option of referring us to someone else. One of the sentences that I think is powerful is *"I'm messaging in case you prefer to communicate this way."* It comes across as thoughtful as well as assumptive. It assumes that the prospect was going to respond and you just wanted to make it easier for them to do so. Additionally, giving the prospect the option of referring us to someone else is great when sending follow-up messages, because it is possible they aren't the right contact. Simply asking for a better contact can motivate the prospect to connect you with someone else, a possible decision maker or stakeholder.

INTERACTING WITH PROSPECTS ON LINKEDIN

Another component of using LinkedIn is interacting with your prospects outside of sending them a message. This typically will come in the form of engaging with their posts or engaging with them in comments. You will have to be connected with the prospect to see these, and typically that would happen if you have connected before in the past. You may be planning on calling them in a few months like they asked. Interacting with their posts is a great way to stay top of mind without coming across salesly. I have two tips for interacting with prospects on LinkedIn.

Tip #1: Never sell.

A comment on a public LinkedIn post is a horrible place to try and book a meeting. The goal of your engagement is to *compliment or add value*. If your prospect posted about a recent company success, congratulate them. If they shared an article about a topic that you're familiar with, add to the conversation. This will keep you on the top of their mind which is important for when the prospect has a need for your product or service before the time that they requested you call back.

Tip #2: Take advantage of groups.

Join groups that are related to the industry, especially when your prospect is a member. Don't just lurk in these groups, contribute. Remember what I said early on in this book? You must become an expert in your industry. Engage in conversations with the goal of adding value, even tag your prospect to get their opinion. This is a great way to learn more about the industry you serve as well as make new connections.

CONCLUSION

You made it through the densest chapter in this book! Feel proud, especially considering that the vast majority of people don't read more than one chapter of any book. I hope that you are walking away from this chapter with a deeper understanding of the prospecting process, about understanding of how sequences work, and how to build one of your own, and how to construct emails and use LinkedIn. Finally, I hope you see how all the different touch points work together to maximize your opportunity of a booked meeting.

APOLLO

While we're on the topic of strategy and tactics, one thing that I'd like to add is that tools can be a very powerful way to execute your strategy. We've discussed how sales engagement platforms can aid you in your prospecting, but one tool that I feel is worth highlighting is Apollo. After using and evaluating multiple tools, I've realized that Apollo is one that has a high potential to help both beginners and experts in outbound sales.

Tools like Apollo keep you organized on a daily basis, and help you gain visibility into where your sales process has the most room for improvement. An interesting thing about Apollo is that it is an all-in-one tool to help you find your target accounts and contacts, enrich your current CRM data, and get in touch with decision makers, by executing on sequences. As mentioned in the previous chapter, sequences allow you to create a repeatable process of reaching out to contacts with multiple touch points over a period of time, including the channels that were covered earlier in this book such as emails, calls, LinkedIn messages, etc.

Sequencing tools are great, but something that sets Apollo apart from the competition is their "*Playbooks*" feature. The major limitation of sequences is that you can only add individual contacts to them, which isn't a big deal if you're only working one to two contacts per account. The challenge is keeping track of all the contacts within each account once you achieve full account penetration, and how each of those accounts is progressing.

The Playbooks feature allows you to add an account into its own Playbook, which will then walk you through a designated process of how to work through that account, and automatically add contacts into the correct sequences based on their titles, seniority levels, and locations. This is all possible because Apollo has a database of 200 million contacts fueling their solution.

This workflow saves a lot of time on the more tedious parts of an Account-Based Sales process, and allows you to stay organized, receive better insights, and dramatically increase productivity. Additionally, using a tool like Apollo to execute your workflow allows you to see which types of market segments and buyer personas your outbound process is working well in. Then, you can use analytics to decide what changes to make to your sales strategy.

If you are choosing to use all of the channels mentioned in this book for your outbound process, Apollo's dialer becomes valuable to your reps. It allows them to stay in one place for prospecting and engagement by simply being able to click on any call task to reach a prospect and then syncing that activity with their CRM. From a coaching perspective, Apollo also records and transcribes your calls so that you can easily search through calls that mention specific topics and always provide your reps with the best learning examples.

We cover email templates in this book but there is an interesting template that Krishan Patel, the Director of Growth at Apollo, shared with me for emails that send out directly after a prospect fails to answer a call. Check it out below.

{{first_name}},

Tried calling you, but you must've been busy.

Thought you might be interested in this article by Harvard Business Review on how to build a great sales force. We help companies with the points around [pieces of the article that are relevant to your solution].

I'll keep trying you over the phone, but please reach out if you have a specific day/time in mind!

Thanks,

{{sender_first_name}}

Finally, I think it is worth mentioning that Apollo has a free data tool which allows you to find new accounts and contacts. The fact that *they give access to their database for free* is one of the main reasons why I felt it was necessary to include them in this book, so that even beginners can take their first step into outbound sales.

Check them out at *https://www.apollo.io* .

METRICS, ORGANIZATION, AND WORKFLOW

METRICS AND IDENTIFYING IMPROVEMENTS

At the core of every sales development rep's role, there's a game of numbers. There are multiple metrics that you can track, which will help illuminate the areas you need to improve. Tracking your own performance is incredibly important because it will give you insight into those areas that you should focus on. Let's look at all the metrics that are relevant to your role as an SDR.

- **Activities** - How many calls, emails, and LinkedIn touches you have made.
- **Connects** - How many decision makers you have connected with.
- **Sets** - How many meetings you have set.
- **Completes** - How many of your meetings took place.
- **Futures** - How many meetings you have scheduled for a later date.
- **SAOs** - How many Sales Accepted Opportunities you have.
- **Closes** - How many of your meetings have closed.

Note 1: These vary in relevance depending on how your company measures SDR performance. Some use sales accepted opportunity (SAO). When the salesperson has agreed that this prospect is a viable sales opportunity that's worth adding to their pipeline. Other companies may evaluate their SDR team on completes, or even closes. You want to closely track up to the point where its relevant to your unique situation.

That being said, you should always keep an eye on how your efforts are impacting the company up stream. Don't just focus on the SAO and move on. Watch that opportunity mature through the sales process and get excited when you see it close. It was your effort that made that opportunity possible!

Note 2: You should also track each outreach method separately—calls, emails, and LinkedIn. That way you can evaluate the effectiveness of each and allocate your time accordingly. For this section I will have these three metrics blended for simplicity, but you should be aware that ideally you would track all methods of outreach individually.

Why are these metrics relevant? Because they tell the story of your effort and help you solve the mystery of your performance. It will also help you understand what you must do in order to achieve the goals you want, so lets walk through an example.

Jamal is a sales development rep at ABC Company and he's trying to achieve 15 SAOs a month, because this is his quota. Last month Jamal missed his quota by 2 SAOs and he has no idea why, since his activity level is high. He tracks his metrics and wants to figure out where he went wrong last month. Here's what he's looking at....

SDR	Activities	Connects	Sets	Completes	SAOs
Jamal	2500	375	60	18	13
Average of Peers	1700	255	46	28	16

What do you see when you look at these metrics? Let's first look at his activity level. Jamal made 2500 activities over the span of a 20 day month—that's 125 activities a day. His peers are accomplishing 85 activities a day, which puts Jamal way above the average in this area. Now let's take a look at his connects—375. Considering both activities and connects, this works out to a 15% connect rate which, compared to Jamal's peers, is pretty average. Not much to note here so let's move onto the next number—sets. He was able to set 60 meetings from those 375 connects and thats a 16% conversion rate, which is about 2% lower than his peers (*let's make a note of that*). The next metric is completes. He had 18 completes last month. This works out to a 30% completion rate, compared to the 45% most of his peers achieve. Are your alarm bells ringing? Lets make sure we check the final metric just to make sure we cover all our bases. He achieved 13 of the 15 SAOs he needed to hit his quota. Those 13 SAOs came from 18 completes which put him at a 72% SAO rate, far above his peers who averaged 60%.

So how should Jamal summarize his performance last month? I would say Jamal is putting in the effort. In a 20 working day month, he is doing 125 activities a day. He could use some help improving his conversion rate to match up with the other reps. Doing this alone would have resulted in 8 more sets, which would have yielded 2 more SAOs and Jamal would have hit his quota of 15 SAOs. That sounds great, but the cause of his conversion being 2% lower than his peers may be tough to pinpoint. It's possible he needs to get better at asking for the meeting, or he might have had a bad week that caused his total conversion rate to be lower than average. Jamal should absolutely try to improve his conversion, but we saw something else that might be an even bigger lever to pull.

Jamal has a 30% set to completion rate, which simply means that the majority of the meetings he sets don't show up. His peers have a 45% completion rate, which forces us to ask the question. *Why?* Jamal speaks to some of his colleagues and realizes that they are calling and sending an email to confirm their meetings. Jamal doesn't, which must be what's causing his show-up rate to be so much lower. What would happen if Jamal achieved the same 45% complete rate as his peers? With all other variables staying the same, Jamal would have ended the month with 19 SAOs, 4 over his quota! Couple this with that 2% increase in conversion rate and Jamal would have ended the month with 22 SAOs, 7 over his quota! Jamal's high activity levels in conjunction with the average connect and complete rate would make him the top SDR at his company!

I hope this illustrates how to use metrics to identify where you may need to improve. Everything we track is designed to give insight into that improvement. Also, looking at these numbers can give alternate ways to achieve your goal. For example, Jamal could have increased the number of activities he was doing daily from 125 to 140. This would have allowed him to hit his quota of 15 SAOs, but might not have been feasible because his activity levels were so much higher than the average already. This will work for you as well. Play with the numbers and decide what metric has the largest impact. If it's realistic to improve that metric, then make that your focus—that will improve your overall results. It's like that super famous quote that everyone knows and loves... *"It's just math."* Ok, maybe that isn't everyone's favorite quote.

ORGANIZING YOUR DAY

One of the most important things you can do to maximize your efficiency is to go into each day with a plan. Doing this will help you avoid letting tasks flow into parts of your day that you should be using for something else. How you organize your day is completely up to you, but you must take into account your productivity levels at specific times. Optimization is always important so your original plan might need to change, depending on the situation. Remember, be flexible.

I'm going to walk you through how to organize your day from my own perspective. You may need to alter some of the suggestions I make to accommodate your personal prospecting needs, productive times, and industry.

I have always been in environments that required a heavy amount of cold calling. I'm a morning person who achieves the highest levels of productivity before noon. I tend to find my creative energy slipping around 3:00pm and completely exhausted by 5:00pm or 6:00pm. However, after 6:00pm I am still able to absorb information effectively enough to retain it. My social abilities stay consistent through the day and anytime I'm awake. If you want to wake me at 2:00am and have a conversation about the probability of the earth being flat, prepare your evidence and I'll make the coffee.

BLOCKING OFF YOUR DAY

The most powerful advice I can give you on the topic of organizing your day is to cherish your mornings. If you are not a morning person you must do everything you can to become one. The morning is the most vital time of the day for multiple reasons. It is often when you will have the most success connecting with your prospects, since there are less distractions, and it will lead to early successes that can jumpstart your day. The morning time is your most valuable so you should use it on tasks that are a top priority.

Typically most cold calls you make will be during the morning because for most people it's when the connect rate is highest. If you have access to that information, I recommend you take a look and see what times during the day you have the highest call to connect rate. This is how you will want to block off your day. For example if you find that connect rates are the highest from 7:00am to 11:00am and 1:00pm to 3:00pm, then you will want to make sure that the only thing you do during those times is make cold calls. This is how your time blocks will start to look.

7:00 AM	**Call Time**	12:30 PM	
7:30 AM	**Call Time**	1:00 PM	**Call Time**
8:00 AM	**Call Time**	1:30 PM	**Call Time**
8:30 AM	**Call Time**	2:00 PM	**Call Time**
9:00 AM	**Call Time**	2:30 PM	**Call Time**
9:30 AM	**Call Time**	3:00 PM	
10:00 AM	**Call Time**	3:30 PM	
10:30 AM	**Call Time**	4:00 PM	
11:00 AM		4:30 PM	
11:30 AM		5:00 PM	
12:00 PM		5:30 PM	

As you can see, this is six hours of cold calling scheduled. This might be too many hours of cold calling, or too few. Go back to the section of this chapter about metrics and use that to estimate how many calls a day you need to make. You will be sending emails and LinkedIn messages as well, but focus on calls for this exercise. Once you have that number, look and see how many calls an hour you would have to make if you dedicated only the hours with the highest call to connect to do your calling. If you came across a number that is possible, then you're in good shape! If you came across a number that would be impossible to make per hour, then you'll need to call during some of the less effective hours to make up the difference.

Cold calling is a high priority task, which is why we started with it. You're most likely not to be calling all day and there should be some free hours. So, what should be your next highest task priority? For most, this will be sending emails. This is less of a priority because emails can be written at any time and scheduled to send in the future. So, unless you need to send an important email ASAP, you can write all your emails at once and then schedule them to send at the time you feel would be the most effective. I suggest writing emails at the end of the day and scheduling them to go out the following morning. Of course, to see if this is right for you, use the data you have available to determine the times with the highest email open rates.

We have plenty of time in the afternoon to write emails if we follow our schedule above. Let's block off some time.

7:00 AM	Call Time	12:30 PM	
7:30 AM	Call Time	1:00 PM	Call Time
8:00 AM	Call Time	1:30 PM	Call Time
8:30 AM	Call Time	2:00 PM	Call Time
9:00 AM	Call Time	2:30 PM	Call Time
9:30 AM	Call Time	3:00 PM	
10:00 AM	Call Time	3:30 PM	Write & Send Emails
10:30 AM	Call Time	4:00 PM	Write & Send Emails
11:00 AM		4:30 PM	Write & Send Emails
11:30 AM		5:00 PM	
12:00 PM		5:30 PM	

An hour and a half should be enough time to send emails if we are following the 3x3 research method we covered in a previous chapter. You may need to adjust this if your prospecting efforts require more emailing.

You may be wondering how to handle the situation when you're on the phone with a prospect and they ask you to send them an email. For the most part, you will want to send this prospect an email at the end of the day, but use good judgment. If you feel that sending the email sooner would benefit you, use your flex time. What is flex time you ask? Flex time is scheduled time where you allow yourself to choose what tasks you work on. Choose an hour that has a low call to connect rate. In our example we choose 11:00am to 12:00pm. This is great for sending out mid-day emails, LinkedIn messages, confirmation calls, or follow-up calls. Think of this as productive free time, like an adult version of recess in elementary school.

If you're responsible for hunting for new accounts and contacts, you will need to schedule that time as well. This is the lowest priority item so save it for the very end of your day, and that, in our example, is from 5:00 pm to 6:00 pm. By having this task saved for the end of the day, you won't sacrifice any productivity and you'll still be able to build your pipeline and stay organized.

Let's take a look at what our day looks like now.

7:00 AM	**Call Time**	12:30 PM	
7:30 AM	**Call Time**	1:00 PM	**Call Time**
8:00 AM	**Call Time**	1:30 PM	**Call Time**
8:30 AM	**Call Time**	2:00 PM	**Call Time**
9:00 AM	**Call Time**	2:30 PM	**Call Time**
9:30 AM	**Call Time**	3:00 PM	
10:00 AM	**Call Time**	3:30 PM	**Write& Send Emails**
10:30 AM	**Call Time**	4:00 PM	**Write & Send Emails**
11:00 AM	**Flex Time**	4:30 PM	**Write & Send Emails**
11:30 AM	**Flex Time**	5:00 PM	**Build/Manage Pipeline**
12:00 PM		5:30 PM	**Build/Manage Pipeline**

Beautiful, isn't it? What's that, LUNCH?! There are calls to make people, so we don't have time for lunch! Alright, the truth is...I love lunch and you should too. It's a pretty high priority task for me, so block off 30 minutes to an hour for it, 12:00 pm to 1:00 pm in our example will work well. You should also take a break or two throughout the day, just to keep your head clear and recharge a bit. I will use 3:00 because that's when I tend to feel the most sluggish. The last thing you may have noticed with our schedule is that it's an 11 hour day. This isn't possible for a lot of people, either because of company policy or burnout. Always take care of your well-being, but I do encourage you to work as hard as you can while in the SDR position. You are building the foundation of your career and that requires a lot of drive and grit. Don't be afraid to push your limits.

HANDLING DISTRACTIONS

Distractions are everywhere, whether it's your colleagues walking around the office, to a bird flying by, or, into the window. Everything and everyone will try and keep you from getting your work done. If you work with a bunch of people who are just as focused and motivated as you, then you're in good shape. The truth is, you will probably end up working with someone who lacks motivation or worse, someone who has such natural ability that they can hit quota and spend half their time walking around the office talking about their favorite waffle house. There are only so many hours in the day and you will need them all. Being in control of your environment will be very important to your success, so make it a priority.

One of the best ways to keep distractions away from you is by making sure that everyone on your team is either following your same schedule or knows your schedule, so they won't bother you. For those who don't follow your schedule, make a sign that you can put up when you're focused. This is a great way to deter visitors, and your coworkers will understand, because, as much as they want to chat with you, they want you to succeed more.

There is one distraction that comes up from time to time that will not only kill your productivity, it will kill your drive.

NEGATIVITY

If there is someone in the office who is very negative, it is important to keep your distance. There is something in sales that I call *"The Virus."* The Virus is a person who is so negative about the job that they infect others with their own beliefs. The problem is that most negativity is intertwined with truth, so it is easy to get "infected" and let it hinder your productivity. I have a firm rule when it comes to negativity, I don't get involved. I don't care how true it seems, I have no interest in complaining about things out of my control. This does not mean to keep your constructive feedback to yourself—quite the contrary. Focus on solutions—that's the constructive piece. If you don't have any solutions, then ignore the negativity and go back to focusing on what you **can** control. If you don't, the negativity will consume you.

PRIORITY NOTETAKING

The most important time to avoid distractions is when you're on the phone with a decision maker. This is the most important part of your day and you need to be laser focused. Something that will help you on the call is taking notes. The challenge most SDRs have is, other than the basic qualifications, they don't know what to write down. The reason why this is tough is because we are listening so hard in order to hear the prospect talk about their need for a solution, that we sometimes forget all the little things they say that could have led us there.

LISTEN CAREFULLY!

Listen to your call recordings and you will hear On Call Alarms that you didn't hear when the call was happening. To help avoid missing opportunities to book a meeting, I developed a note-taking system that helps keep track of what the prospect says and prioritizes what to talk about next. I call this method *Priority Notetaking.*

Priority notetaking is a method of notetaking where the goal is to prioritize what to talk about next while keeping your mind open to take in new information. Often times while an SDR is on a call with a decision maker, they will get excited about something they heard that they feel is the path that will lead to a booked meeting. What can happen is that the SDR may miss other important pieces of information, because their brain is so focused on the first thing. The problem occurs when the prospect says something that's more powerful than the first thing the SDR heard. This can lead to a missed opportunity.

PRIORITY NOTETAKING STEPS

The first step of this process is to write down what the prospect says that you believe is important and could guide the conversation in a direction of a booked meeting. Once you have that written down circle it with your pen and don't stop circling. Let your hand continue to circle those words or phrases while you free your mind to pay attention to what else the prospect is saying. When the prospect says something else that you find important to write down, go ahead and write it down. Once you have written that word or phrase, make a decision about which one you feel is a better direction for you to take the call. Start circling that one, keep circling and free your mind again. Keep doing this until the prospect is done speaking and when you take a look at your notes, what to do will become obvious.

Take the call in the direction of the word or phrase with the most circles around it. This is a very simple concept that, in practice, does an incredible job freeing your mind from the pressure of trying to remember what to say next. Allowing you to listen better without sacrificing your ability to keep track of what you feel the best direction to take the call is.

Log everything

Sales operation analysts everywhere are rejoicing because this section is in the book. Salespeople are notorious for not logging calls accurately...or at all. There are many reasons why this is the case:

- the rep is really busy and forgot
- they think it's a waste of time

Regardless of the reason, there is no excuse for not logging your calls. Having a record of each of your calls, even the unsuccessful ones, gives you insight on how to approach your accounts. To be clear, not developing the habit of logging everything will impact your success. With that said, I do understand that it can take some time to do this.

I want to share a way to shorten the notes you write. First, let's look at a common example of a note.

Note: I spoke with the director of customer success, Lisa, and she said that they have had trouble getting their customer support team to complete tickets. There's a lot of missing information. She seemed interested in our solution, but is too busy to look at it now. She asked that I send an email and follow up next month.

The good thing about this note is that it tells us what happened. The not so good thing is that it uses more words than necessary—59 words to be exact. Becoming more efficient with note taking will save you time writing and reading. It's not an insignificant amount of time either—roughly, 8 hours a month if you are making 80 calls a day.

If we can cut that in half than you just bought yourself a half a day in extra time each month. That half a day could be the difference between hitting your quota or missing it by one.

Remember...it's a numbers game.

Let's take a look of the same note done in a more efficient way.

Note: DM, Lisa - Challenge getting CS team to complete tickets, tickets missing info - seemed interested - requested email and callback next month.

This note says the exact same thing in 20 words and that's 66% less time spent typing. Notice that one way we accomplish this is by using some abbreviations. We are taking advantage of common abbreviations for "decision maker" and customer success. I want to make a point to mention that we are not creating our own language. You do not need to abbreviate everything, but take advantage of what you can abbreviate. Here's a few abbreviations that you can take advantage of.

VM: Left a voicemail

LM: Left a message with a gatekeeper

NA: No answer/no message left

GK: Spoke with a gatekeeper

DM: Spoke with the decision maker (should include follow-up notes about the content of the call)

NDM: Spoke with someone who isn't the decision maker (should include notes as well)

FOLLOWING UP

As you build and manage your pipeline you will find yourself making more and more follow-up calls. This is great! It means that you are doing a great job building interest. Not everyone will be willing to schedule a meeting on the first call, even if they are interested in your solution. People have priorities and just because they were blessed by your cold call doesn't mean they will drop everything. These follow-up calls will be the key to your success month after month, as long as you keep your activity up and your pipeline full. In this section we are going to cover the difference between warm and cold follow-ups, when to follow up, and what your messaging should be.

WARM VS. COLD FOLLOW UP

As I write this, I have the space heater running in my office. You see, I like my office the way I like my prospects—warm and toasty! However, follow ups are not all created equal. How you approach each depends greatly on your previous conversations.

So, what is the main difference between a warm and a cold prospect?

INTEREST

The more interested the prospect, the warmer the follow-up. Take a look at the definition of each, specifically as it relates to the account.

> **Warm follow up accounts:**You spoke with the decision maker or stakeholder who expressed a problem that your product or service solves and demonstrated interest.

> **Cold follow up accounts:**You spoke with a decision maker or stakeholder who expressed a problem that your product or service solves and demonstrated a lack of interest.

COLD ACCOUNTS

As you can imagine, the way you follow up with each of these accounts is very different. We are going to start with cold follow up accounts. The two variables that come into play are who told you that they weren't interested and why they told you that. Remember, we are working multiple contacts at each account. If one of your contacts is a stakeholder who you would consider less involved in the decision making process, you will want to take their feedback with a grain of salt. Just because they said that they aren't interested doesn't mean that everyone in the company is also not interested. The good news is that we found out that they do have a problem. Let's take a look at what this workflow would be like.

> **Step 1:** Remove the uninterested contact from our sequence.

> **Step 2:** Add another contact to a follow up sequence.

> **Step 3:** Leverage what you learned from the uninterested contact to schedule a meeting with the new contact.

Understanding Step 3

Steps one and two are pretty self-explanatory, so let's dive into step 3. We learned that they have a problem that we can solve from our previous conversation with a stakeholder. We will be using this information to build credibility early in the call with the new contact, so lets take a look at an example introduction.

> SDR: **Hi Michelle, this is Kyle from ABC Company, how's it going?**
> Prospect: **Good**

SDR: **Great, I'm reaching out because I spoke with Kevin and he told me that a challenge your team faces is collecting all the data from each marketing channel, in order to determine which channels are the most effective. I'm not sure if we can help each other, but I thought it was worth a quick call. Mind if I ask you a couple questions and let you decide if we should chat?**

Prospect: **Sure**

Leveraging someone else in the organization is a great way to get your new contact's attention. Of course, we didn't mention that Kevin said that he wasn't interested; we will let our new contact evaluate for herself. The next part of this interaction would typically be giving a path, but we already know that there's a problem, so we have the opportunity to take a shortcut. Let's continue with our example.

Prospect: **Sure**

SDR: **Thanks for the time. I'm calling from ABC Company. We give tech companies the ability to collect data from multiple lead sources and evaluate their effectiveness. When I spoke to Kevin he said this is a challenge for your company. I'm curious, how does this impact you specifically?**

By moving the conversation towards the impact, their challenge allows us to understand our prospects situation, find the gap, and book the meeting. Now, you might not be successful in scheduling this meeting; maybe the decision maker wants an email. That's fine, because you turned a cold follow-up call into a future warm one. I would consider that a success.

Now, what if you cannot get in touch with the new contact? Maybe this is why you ended up speaking with a stakeholder that was far removed from the decision-making process in the first place. In this situation we will have to use email and LinkedIn to get their attention. Fortunately, the messaging for this is very similar. Take a look at the example below.

Hi Michelle,

I spoke with Kevin and he told me that a challenge your team faces is collecting all the data from each marketing channel in order to determine which are most effective.

Our tool allows tech companies to collect data from multiple lead sources and evaluate their effectiveness with an instant ROI calculation resulting in a 15% increase in ROI. If this resonates we should set up a quick call. Do you have some time tomorrow at 11am?

Best,

Kyle

_____

This is very similar to the emails we constructed in a previous chapter. The main change is instead of using our research to create a tailored introduction, we use our conversation with the other contact that we spoke with. This should have an even more powerful effect because we know about their organization's specific problems. The goal here is to leverage what we can in order to turn this cold follow up account to a warm account. Once we have generated some interest we must react by changing our approach.

WARM ACCOUNTS

If you've spoken with a decision maker or stakeholder and they've admitted to a problem and are interested in your solution, that account would be considered a warm account. If you were unable to schedule a meeting, then you will need to follow up with that prospect. The process of following up with a warm account is different than that of a cold one. In a previous chapter, we spoke about sending emails every three weeks with blog post and other materials that add value. Eventually, the day will come that you will need to pick up the phone and call that person. In this section we will talk about when you should make that call, how you should approach that call, and how to use email if your calls go unanswered.

Because you know there is a need for your product or service, as well as an interest, these calls are typically fun to make. If you've been sending those value emails every three weeks like we spoke about in chapter 8, then making this call will be a breeze.

When to Call

The first question is when you should make that call. When you originally had a conversation with the contact, odds are they gave you a broad time frame for a follow up. They may have asked you to call them back next quarter or in a few months. My suggestion is to call anywhere from *one to four weeks before they asked you to*. The decision between one week and four is made based on the amount of time since you spoke. For example, if it's January and the prospect says "call me around October" calling them in September would be fine. If the prospect asked for a call in February calling them the last week in January to set up that call is appropriate. The only reason to bypass this rule would be if the prospect had a specific reason for the timing of your call. For example, the prospect tells you that they are hiring a new marketing director and they start in March.

When it is time to make that call, you want to be as assumptive as possible. Make the process of scheduling a meeting with you very simple and easy. We have done our best to mitigate the risk of receiving an objection by sending value emails every three weeks. Still, the prospect may give you an objection. If this happens, use the techniques from the chapter on objection handling and have a conversation with them about the importance of solving their problem. Let's take a look at an introduction we can use with a contact from a warm account.

> SDR: **Hi Michelle. It's Kyle from ABC Company, How've you been?**
>
> Prospect: **I've been great Kyle, how about you?**
>
> SDR: **I've been wonderful, thanks for asking. Last time we spoke you were having trouble collecting data from each of your marketing channels, so you weren't able to see their effectiveness. I caught you in the middle of board meeting prep and you asked that we set something up for early September to talk about solving this. I know I caught you out of the blue today. Do you have some time this week for a call? How would 11am tomorrow work?**

This introduction is designed to get right to the point and book the meeting. If you built good rapport with the prospect, you should bring that up. For example, if the they had told you they had a fishing trip coming up, ask them how that trip went. Your goal is to remind the prospect of the previous call and leverage that positive interaction to motivate them to schedule a meeting. After a strong introduction we remind the prospect of the problem that they are experiencing and that we are calling to talk about a solution. We then follow that up with an assumptive ask for a meeting. Keep the call simple and the prospect will as well. This isn't a cold call, because you've already established a relationship.

There is no need to over-complicate a simple scheduling call.

Email to warm account

You are going to find yourself in a situation where the prospect you are trying to follow up with won't answer their phone. You guessed it! We will need to use other means of communication—email and LinkedIn. The email we are sending will be much like the one we sent to our cold account, except we get to spice it up a bit.

Take a look at the example below.

Hi Michelle,

It's been awhile since we last spoke, about a month or so. I hope you had an awesome time on that fishing trip with the kids, Alaska is beautiful.

Last time we spoke you were having trouble collecting data from each of your marketing channels so you weren't able to see their effectiveness. You asked me to reach out in September and set up a meeting to show you how we help. When would be a good time to chat this week?

Best,

Kyle   -------

This is a simple email that reminds the prospect of your previous conversation. Much like our call script, our goal is to attempt to book this meeting by leveraging our previous conversation. When we send this email, we should also plan to have more follow-up emails as part of our sequence. Often, people forget to respond to emails, so we don't want to assume a lack of interest when we don't get a response. First, try the simple reminder email that we have in our main sequence. If that doesn't get a response, we can send another email that nudges the prospect to respond. Take a look at this example of an email following up on a call.

Hi Michelle,

Sorry I missed you on the phone today. I was giving you a ring to continue our conversation about improving your data collection so you can accurately calculate the ROI of each of your marketing channels.

When would be a good time for us to chat this week?

Best,

Kyle   -------

Don't expect all warm accounts to schedule a meeting when you reach out to them at the time they asked. Solving the specific challenge that you are reaching out to them about is one of many tasks on the prospect's plate. You will have to continue to pursue these accounts until they show up to a meeting, so make sure you keep a good relationship.

CONFIRMING MEETINGS

We have covered many topics in this chapter. Some, more complex than others. This final section is about rescheduling meetings that didn't show up. It's bound to happen. You spend so much time working an account and you finally book a meeting with the decision maker! After all that effort, you need to do everything in your power to make sure that they show up to their meeting.

Control the Controllables!

CONFIRMING YOUR MEETINGS
Take a look at the process at a high level and then, discuss each step.

- ✓ **Step 1:** Meeting set email
- ✓ **Step 2:** Calendar invite
- ✓ **Step 3a:** Call to confirm day before
- ✓ **Step 3b:** Email to confirm day before (if the call was unsuccessful)
- ✓ **Step 4a:** Reminder email
- ✓ **Step 4b:** Call to confirm (if unable to confirm)

MEETING SET EMAIL
Once you have successfully scheduled a meeting, you should send a recap email to the prospect. This is helpful because they will have an easy way to get ahold of you if they need to reschedule. The other benefit is that it comes across as professional, which increases the perceived importance of the meeting. Finally, it will remind the prospect of the value of the next call. Following, you will see an example of what this email should look like.

Subject: Great chatting today!

Hi Michele,

It was a pleasure speaking with you today. Thanks for the time. I have spoken with Taylor, our product specialist. I let her know that you are looking for a way to easily evaluate the ROI of each of your marketing channels. Taylor is looking forward to walking you through how we can help this **Thursday 11/8 at 11:00 am PST.** In the meantime, don't hesitate to respond with any questions that you might have.

Best,

Kyle ⎯⎯⎯⎯⎯

CALENDAR INVITE

The next step is to send the prospect a calendar invitation. This will block that time off on their calendar, as well as remind them that they have a meeting with you. Use the subject line field to remind the prospect of the reason why they set the meeting. Take a look at the example below.

> **Subject:** Your Company: XYZ Company's marketing channels ROI calculation

CALL/EMAIL THE DAY BEFORE

The next step starts off with a phone call to confirm the meeting the day before it's scheduled for. You may want to consider calling two days before if you booked this meeting an unusually long time ago. The purpose of this call is to get a quick confirmation that the prospect will show up to their meeting. Read through the script below.

> SDR: **Hi Michelle, its Kyle from ABC company how've you been?**
>
> Prospect: **I've been great, how about you?**
>
> SDR: **I'm doing excellent thanks for asking. I am calling because we have a meeting on the calendar tomorrow at 11am and I wanted to check and see if there's anything you need from me before tomorrow?**

This short script is effective because we aren't giving the prospect an "out" by asking them if the time still works. Instead we are giving the prospect the opportunity to let us know if they can't make it, as well as offering help if needed.

Not all prospects are easy to contact over the phone and, in this situation, we must resort to email. Take a look at the simple confirmation email below. Notice it is direct, making it easy for the prospect to respond to.

Hi Michelle,

I am reaching out to confirm our meeting for tomorrow at 11am. Taylor is looking forward to walking you through how we can help you collect the data from all your marketing channels so you can better evaluation the ROI of each.

Does tomorrow still work for you?

Best,

Kyle

FINAL CONFIRMATION CALL/EMAIL

If you haven't been able to connect with the prospect and confirm the meeting, you should call them the day of the meeting as well. The goal is the same as the confirmation call we covered earlier in this section. Confirm the meeting a day before, then follow up with a reminder email. This is a simple way to keep the meeting fresh on the prospect's mind. Take a look at the example below.

Hello Michelle,

I hope your day is off to a wonderful start. I'm looking forward to connecting today at 11am!

Best,

Kyle

RESCHEDULING MEETINGS

I have a sad story for you folks. There will be a time in every SDRs career, where they do everything right and the prospect doesn't show up. This can be devastating, especially if they had high hopes that the meeting was going to go well. When this happens to you, *don't be disappointed*, because it's part of the job. Instead, embark on the journey to reschedule that meeting. We've already covered the sequence you use to reschedule a meeting. Let's cover a script that you can use along with an email template.

The Script

SDR: **Hi Michelle, Its Kyle from ABC Company, how's it going?**

Prospect: **it's going well, how are you?**

SDR: **I'm doing great thanks for asking. It looks like our wires got crossed yesterday and we weren't able to connect. I wanted to reach out and reschedule that for you. What does your calendar look like tomorrow at the same time, 11am?**

There are typically two things that happen on a confirmation call: the prospect will interrupt you with an apology or they will interrupt you with an objection. If they apologize, go ahead and reschedule the meeting. If they interrupt with an objection, use the techniques that we covered in the chapter about objection handling.

Sometimes the prospect is dodging your calls out of embarrassment or lack of interest. If this is the case, we must resort to email in an attempt to get this meeting back on the books. When constructing this email it is important to make sure the prospect doesn't feel bad about not showing up to the meeting. Take a look at the example below.

Hello Michelle!

I'm so sorry, it seems like our wires got crossed the other day and we weren't able to connect. I hope I didn't get the time mixed up! Taylor was going to walk you through how we can help you collect the data from all your marketing channels so you can better evaluate the ROI of each.

I'm happy to reschedule this meeting, when would be the best time for you this week?

Best,

Kyle

CONCLUSION

You did it! You made it to the end of a long chapter with a lot of information in it. Metrics, organization, and workflow are all very important for being a successful sales development representative. If you neglect your metrics you will not be able to react quickly when it's necessary. For example, if you are experiencing a meeting show rate of 25% when your average is 50%, you must change your tactics to make up for that deficit. If you never see that metric, you may find yourself missing your quota and wondering *"How is this possible? I put in the same effort as last month."* To continue with our example, knowing that your show rate has dropped will allow you to increase your activities to make up for the loss in meeting rate, as well as put more energy in making sure your meetings show up. Remember, this is a numbers game.

You need to know your numbers!

Being organized is challenging for most people; you may have to work hard at it. This is a <u>mandatory</u> skill and necessary in all areas of sales. As you work more complex deals and have more prospects in your pipeline, you will find it harder to remember everything about all of your prospects. Be diligent everyday to improve your organization and prevent things from slipping through the cracks.

Finally, there's workflow. This area will improve as you continue to strategically organize and execute. Mastering your activities will allow you to be more effective with the time you spend. The bulk of that time should be spent on activities that will *"move the needle"* and get you closer to hitting your quota. Mastering other tasks that eat up valuable time will allow you to execute those tasks quickly and get back to more impactful activities.

Metrics, organization, and workflow are all incredibly important for competentcy. All of these are used simultaneously to aid you in hitting your quota consistently. Consistently is the key word here. Anyone can hit quota on any given month. What is challenging is hitting quota *every* month and every quarter. If you are able to do that you, will be invaluable as an SDR.

Metrics, organization, and workflow are there to help you become consistent.

So...Master them!

10

STRIVE TO BE THE BEST

If there is something that is often lacking in the sales development world, I would say it's passion. There are, of course, people who are passionate about helping sales development reps achieve success and advance their careers. Unfortunately, there are not that many sales development reps who are passionate about the role itself. For most people, the SDR role is the path to achieve more success in their careers. It's a launchpad for better things to come. Because of this most reps are pushing themselves as hard as they can to get out of the role as fast as possible.

Is that a good thing? I will admit, I'm not sure. On one hand, the motivation to make it to the next chapter in one's career can be exactly the motivator necessary to do a killer job as a sales development rep. On the other, a lack of passion actually hinders one's ability to master a skill that will provide value to them throughout their career, regardless if it's in sales or not.

I know phenomenal salespeople who were unbelievably gifted SDRs. They made statements so loud that their previous companies still talk about them. I also know phenomenal salespeople who did a lackluster jobs as an SDR, but got promoted because it was a small company that needed someone to sell for them. They were in the right place at the right time.

I'm sure great salespeople come from a wide range of backgrounds. I'm not sure what kind of background would have served me the best, because I can't go back and change my background to see the result. This causes me to resort back to my default philosophy—*do what has the highest chance of a successful result,* even if there is another potential way to achieve it with less effort. I guess that's just a complicated way of saying...

Always play full out!

The journey you are on is a sacred one, because its yours. You choose how to navigate the maze that is life. A big portion of that maze is your career—your work life. Will you experience failure? Of course. Will you find yourself in a position where success looks impossible? Absolutely.

The solutions to these events won't come easy in many cases, but they all require the same thing to solve—*You*.

The reason why I advocate for playing full out is because I believe that's what it takes to prevail in times of difficulty. Odds are, if you are reading this book and made it this far, you play full out. This will serve you well, because with that mentality, you will empower yourself to make decisions clearly and without having to settle for wherever you might land.

Often times, through the experience of failure, people end up settling for something undesirable. If you get knocked off a ledge and it was a far drop, what happens? Well, you're hurt; you probably can't move at first. All your energy is channeled into standing back up.

Once you do stand and get comfortable, it's very easy to stay where you landed, metaphorically speaking.

There's a huge benefit to pushing past that initial desire to stay comfortable, because as a successful SDR, you can go on to achieve a lot. Often when we think of someone in the SDR role, we think of someone who has a desire to be in sales. In practice, the progression of a sales development representative is much more diverse than one might think.

More and more companies are having the sales development team report to the marketing department. In some cases this has resulted in a marketing focus for many SDR teams, working inbound leads and following up on trade show leads etc. This relationship has opened doors for SDR reps to move into more of a marketing function. In addition, we are seeing more and more former SDRs leading customer success teams because of their knowledge of the end user and their ability to communicate effectively over the phone—both valuable in ensuring a positive experience for any organization's customers.

With the rise of UX design as a field, we are starting to see SDRs move from their development positions into UX design research roles and this opens up an entirely new career path for those individuals.

The ability to effectively communicate the value of a product or service transcends sales, but sales is still a strong progressive path for an SDR and by far, the most "paved."

Sales isn't for everyone, but everyone is for sales. What I mean by that is regardless of your role, you are involved in articulating value. No one articulates value better than salespeople. It's their job; it's what they work to master. This is why the role of an SDR is such a valuable one. It builds a strong foundation in the articulation of value.

> *This foundation will serve you well*
> *as you learn and grow as a professional.*

I love the SDR role. I love working with people early in their careers or those who are transitioning to another industry. They are all starting a new chapter in their careers as an SDR. It's a time of growth. Facilitating that growth is something I'm incredibly passionate about. I've put a lot of effort into this book, completely rewriting the first version.

The reason is because I want to have a positive impact on as many people as possible. Some will read this book and feel that they know a better way. They might even be right! My only claim is to have a way that has worked for me and the SDRs I have trained.

The role of a sales development rep is challenging and a lot of people quit. Unfortunately, not all SDRs have good guidance from mentors to help them succeed.

I hope that, by reading this book, you are able to find success. If you do, pay it forward and support others on their own journey. Regardless of where you are in your life remember...

> *You're just getting started!*

INDEX